Reconstructing
UKRAINE

CREATING A FREER, MORE PROSPEROUS, AND SECURE FUTURE

Howard J. Shatz, Gabrielle Tarini,
Charles P. Ries, James Dobbins

RAND NATIONAL DEFENSE RESEARCH INSTITUTE

On the Cover

The Ukrainian stamps shown on the front and back covers are from a block of stamps released by Ukrposhta, Ukraine's National Post, on February 15, 2023. Designed by Oleksandr Nikityuk, they are called "Warriors of light. Warriors of good" ("Воїни світла. Воїни добра"). They honor the workers who restore infrastructure in Ukraine after Russian missile attacks.

For more information on this publication, visit **www.rand.org/t/RRA2200-1**.

About RAND

The RAND Corporation is a research organization that develops solutions to public policy challenges to help make communities throughout the world safer and more secure, healthier and more prosperous. RAND is nonprofit, nonpartisan, and committed to the public interest. To learn more about RAND, visit www.rand.org.

Research Integrity

Our mission to help improve policy and decisionmaking through research and analysis is enabled through our core values of quality and objectivity and our unwavering commitment to the highest level of integrity and ethical behavior. To help ensure our research and analysis are rigorous, objective, and nonpartisan, we subject our research publications to a robust and exacting quality-assurance process; avoid both the appearance and reality of financial and other conflicts of interest through staff training, project screening, and a policy of mandatory disclosure; and pursue transparency in our research engagements through our commitment to the open publication of our research findings and recommendations, disclosure of the source of funding of published research, and policies to ensure intellectual independence. For more information, visit www.rand.org/about/principles.

RAND's publications do not necessarily reflect the opinions of its research clients and sponsors.

Published by the RAND Corporation, Santa Monica, Calif.
© 2023 RAND Corporation
RAND® is a registered trademark.

Library of Congress Cataloging-in-Publication Data is available for this publication.

ISBN: 978-1-9774-1142-6

Cover design by Rick Penn-Kraus; stamps: A_Gree/Alamy stock photo; brick wall: Joanna Ciesielska/Getty Images/iStockphoto; flag: Getty Images.

About This Report

The economic and social damage of Russia's war on Ukraine has been devastating. The conflict is ongoing, but it is not too early to begin to plan for the country's post-war reform and reconstruction. This report is intended to help gauge the dimensions of Ukraine's reform and reconstruction and suggest a strategy to ensure its success. To orient U.S. policymakers to the practical dimensions of Ukraine's reconstruction, this analysis draws on lessons from relevant historical examples of post-war reconstruction and insights from post-disaster reconstruction. It provides concrete insights on how to organize and finance Ukraine's reform and reconstruction and situates reconstruction in the context of the need for durable post-war security arrangements. We expect that this analysis will help U.S. officials to prepare and plan for a long-term, consistent U.S. policy toward Ukraine and Europe more broadly.

RAND National Security Research Division

This research was conducted within the International Security and Defense Policy Program of the RAND National Security Research Division (NSRD), which operates the RAND National Defense Research Institute (NDRI), a federally funded research and development center (FFRDC) sponsored by the Office of the Secretary of Defense, the Joint Staff, the Unified Combatant Commands, the Navy, the Marine Corps, the defense agencies, and the defense intelligence enterprise. This research was made possible by NDRI exploratory research funding that was provided through the FFRDC contract and approved by NDRI's primary sponsor.

For more information on the RAND International Security and Defense Policy Program, see www.rand.org/nsrd/isdp or contact the director (contact information is provided on the webpage.

Acknowledgments

We thank our formal reviewers, William Courtney and William Taylor, for their thoughtful comments, which greatly strengthened the report. We also thank Shelly Culbertson, Gary Edson, Douglas Lute, and Robert Zoellick for their informal reviews and many valuable suggestions, and Lisa Saum-Manning for a review of an earlier draft, all of which helped us strongly improve the report. Matt Byrd piloted the manuscript through the RAND publication process, Rachel Ostrow provided expert editing, Rick Penn-Kraus designed the cover, and Sandy Petitjean prepared the figures. All errors of fact and interpretation are those of the authors.

Summary

Post-war reconstruction in Ukraine may be the largest rebuilding effort in modern history. The United States and Europe have started to plan for its success. Over the past 75 years, they have been engaged in multiple reconstruction efforts. Drawing lessons from the most appropriate of these efforts will be important for planning Ukraine's reform and reconstruction.

In this century, the most notable U.S. reconstruction efforts were in Iraq and Afghanistan, but these are not the right models. Ukraine is fundamentally different. When the fighting slows, there is unlikely to be an insurgency or civil war. More-relevant lessons can be drawn from the truly transformative rebuilding of Western Europe after World War II, Eastern Europe after the Cold War, and the Western Balkans after the violent break-up of Yugoslavia. The basic formula for these reconstruction efforts was set early on. The United States provided seed money and security, while the Europeans provided the bulk of the funding and advanced the historic process of European integration.

Security Is Essential for Ukraine's Reconstruction

Without security, reconstruction will falter. Durable security gives businesses and investors the confidence to take risks and make long-term commitments. The North Atlantic Treaty Organization (NATO) provided security for European reconstruction after World War II and the Cold War and deployed more than 100,000 peacekeepers to Bosnia, Kosovo, Croatia, and Macedonia after the break-up of Yugoslavia. Security for post-war Ukraine will be as essential.

Once the fighting ends, the promise of reconstruction assistance and European Union (EU) membership will give Ukraine powerful positive incentives to keep the peace. Russia will not be offered any comparable benefits. Its adherence to peace will have to rest principally on deterrence.

This could take a variety of forms. The United States and its allies can promise to perpetuate current arrangements for the provision of Western arms, ammunition, training, and advice. They also could threaten or even promise to introduce Western forces into Ukraine if Russia reattacks. Or they could bring Ukraine into NATO.

While stronger measures of deterrence might make renewed fighting less likely, they could also raise Russia's threat perceptions, potentially leading Moscow to take desperate measures. And, if deterrence fails, the resultant conflict would be less likely to be limited to Ukraine.

Arrangements for Ukraine's security might require new models. Europe's security architecture has long offered states a binary choice: A country is in NATO or it is not. Policymakers should evaluate alternatives for Ukraine, which has never quite fit into this model.

Lessons from Post-War and Post–Natural Disaster Reconstruction

The United States played a leading role in Europe's 75-year post-war reconstruction. It also has often been central in response to large-scale natural disasters. Similar to war, these disasters feature significant destruction of physical infrastructure and socio-economic systems. Lessons for Ukraine's reconstruction can be drawn from the aftermaths of both wars and natural disasters.

Organizing Ukraine's reconstruction should be decided in advance. There are a few simple principles: Ukraine should set priorities. The United States should spearhead security, and the EU should spearhead economic recovery. But both the United States and the countries of Europe will need to be involved with security and economic recovery.

After the fall of the Berlin Wall and the freeing of Central and Eastern Europe, the U.S. Congress gave a single senior coordinator broad oversight powers. Replicating this for Ukraine will aid the U.S. reconstruction effort. The United States, Europe, and multilateral agencies should have senior officials on the ground in Kyiv in daily contact with Ukrainian authorities; periodic donor conferences are insufficient.

Ukraine reconstruction will need a strong, trusted inspector general to safeguard the integrity of assistance, especially given Kyiv's record of corruption since gaining independence in 1991. International donors should, in parallel, institute effective monitoring and be ready to halt funding if corruption emerges.

The sequencing and prioritizing of essential tasks—de-mining, rubble clearance, building shelter and schools, providing basic medical care—is needed to jump-start reconstruction and help people return. Aid conditionality is important, as are the prospects of EU membership and economic integration for trade and investment. Reconstruction efforts must solicit and address local priorities. The millions of internally displaced persons and refugees will not return organically, so policymakers will need to facilitate returns.

To pay for reform and reconstruction, international aid, private financing, and Ukraine's own resources are needed. Aid historically has provided a relatively small amount of the total but, importantly, attracts other funding and serves as risk capital when the private sector is reluctant. Russian assets, both official and private, could be significant parts of support to Ukraine, although using them will require strong legal justifications and could raise longer-term systemic risks both to the centrality of the U.S. financial system in global finance and to dollar dominance.

Sustaining Public Support for Reconstruction

Ukraine's recovery could take decades. Enduring public support will be vital. In 1948, President Harry Truman's administration and congressional leaders embarked on a well-coordinated, bipartisan effort to gain public approval for the Marshall Plan, the archetypal post-war reconstruction effort. Although the Marshall Plan stands out, in retrospect, as a great success, its approval was not at all certain. The United States will need a similar public strategy for Ukraine.

Implications for Action

Developing plans for, contributing to, and overseeing Ukraine's reconstruction will be a complex process; course corrections are certain as implementation starts and continues. But the United States has three priority actions even before the shooting in Russia's war on Ukraine stops.

First, U.S. policymakers need to carefully examine alternatives, both old and new, for Ukrainian security in preparation for engaging with allies. This will be crucial to every other aspect of reconstruction.

Second, the administration and Congress should approve a modern version of the laws that enabled U.S. activities in Central and Eastern Europe and the former Soviet Union after the Cold War—the Support for East European Democracy (SEED) Act and the Freedom for Russia and Emerging Eurasian Democracies and Open Markets (FREEDOM) Support Act. A new law will set the basis for organizing the U.S. effort and create the position of empowered coordinator, as was created in the past, to deal with European governments, international financial institutions, and the people and government in Ukraine. The new law should include both an inspector general and a monitoring and evaluation mechanism.

Third, the entire future course of Ukraine's reconstruction will benefit from the development and implementation of a bipartisan effort to explain and build support among the American people for a longer-term U.S. policy in Ukraine. Such support cannot be taken for granted.

The challenge of reforming and reconstructing Ukraine after Russia's full-scale invasion in February 2022 should be seen in light of Europe's successful post-war record and the consistent, 75-year security and economic policies of the United States. Security and reconstruction will go hand in hand, as they did after World War II. When the Marshall Plan was being formed, the participation of all of Europe, including the Soviet Union, was deemed possible, but the Soviet Union blocked such participation. A secure, economically prosperous Ukraine that is fully integrated into European institutions will be a capstone achievement, bringing to fruition the multi-generation European project built on the foundations of an enduring trans-Atlantic partnership.

Contents

Figures and Table

Figures

Table

CHAPTER 1

Introduction

The conflict in Ukraine is ongoing, violent, and destructive. Yet it is not too early to begin planning for the country's post-war reform and reconstruction. This report is intended to help gauge the dimensions of Ukraine's reconstruction and suggest a strategy to ensure its success. In the case of Ukraine, this will include not only recovery and reconstruction from the war, but a reform effort in the wake of 40 years of economic and political underperformance.

It is worth recalling that the U.S. role in post-war reconstruction and nation-building was a justifiable source of national pride before it became the target of opprobrium. After World War II (WWII), Japan, Germany, and the rest of Western Europe were transformed with the aid of U.S. assistance, as was South Korea subsequently.[1] The record of U.S. reconstruction and nation-building activity over the 30 years following the end of the Cold War has been more mixed. Post-war reconstruction efforts often turned into grinding counterinsurgency campaigns. This has been the bitter experience in Somalia, Haiti, Afghanistan, and Iraq as the United States and others sought to help weak and divided states emerging from civil wars build peaceful societies and functioning states.[2]

But Ukraine's reform and reconstruction will little resemble the post-conflict missions of the 21st century. Ukraine mounted a ferocious defense to Russia's February 2022 invasion, proving itself neither weak nor divided.

---

[1] Benn Steil, *The Marshall Plan: The Dawn of the Cold War*, Oxford University Press, 2018; David C. Cole and Princeton N. Lyman, *Korean Development: The Interplay of Politics and Economics*, Harvard University Press, 1971.

[2] James Dobbins, John G. McGinn, Keith Crane, Seth G. Jones, Rollie Lal, Andrew Rathmell, Rachel M. Swanger, and Anga R. Timilsina, *America's Role in Nation-Building: From Germany to Iraq*, RAND Corporation, MR-1753-RC, 2003.

Nor will Ukraine be emerging from a civil war, which comes with the risk of residual dissatisfied elements resisting and forming an insurgency. Ukraine will be emerging from an interstate conflict in which the enemy is exterior rather than interior. Therefore, the post-war reconstruction challenges in Ukraine are unlikely to resemble the challenges that Washington faced in Iraq and Afghanistan and continues to address globally in other fragile states that are vulnerable to intrastate violence. Rather, Ukraine's reconstruction is more likely to resemble the European experience with post-war reconstruction: the rebuilding of Europe after WWII, the post–Cold War transformation of the countries of Eastern Europe from communist dictatorships into free-market democracies, and reconstruction efforts in the Western Balkans after the wars that accompanied the breakup of Yugoslavia. Likewise, given the level of destruction in Ukraine, parallels can be drawn with post-disaster reconstruction.

The basic formula that gave success to the Marshall Plan has continued to yield positive results in the post–Cold War era; first, in the transformation of the states of Central and Eastern Europe from communist dictatorships into market democracies, and then in the enduring peace settlements that ended the Western Balkan wars. In all three instances, the United States was a major initiator of the changes and the largest single contributor, but Europe was the principal designer and eventually the largest funder of these transformations. This pattern was set from the beginning when the United States offered to provide initial funding for Europe's rebuilding, provided that European governments agreed among themselves on a common approach.[3] The United States bankrolled the Marshall Plan, but the Europeans themselves did much of the planning, and over the life of the program the countries of Europe did it effectively together.

European integration was the glue that held post-war reconstruction together, giving it purpose and long-term durability. The Marshall Plan gave a major impetus to the process of European integration, beginning with the creation of the European Coal and Steel Community (1951), the European Economic Community (1957, later renamed the European Com-

---

[3] J. Bradford De Long and Barry Eichengreen, "The Marshall Plan: History's Most Successful Structural Adjustment Program," National Bureau of Economic Research, Working Paper No. 3899, November 1991.

munity), the European Union (EU) (1993), the European Monetary Union (involving adoption of the euro by a subset of EU members, 1999), and the entry of nine former Warsaw Pact and Soviet Union states.[4] The reforms needed to qualify for EU membership became the template for the transformation of these former communist dictatorships.[5] This is the future for which reconstruction should prepare Ukraine, which, although no longer communist, still faces challenging reform tasks.

Ukraine will begin the next phase of its history with numerous disadvantages. It will have been the setting for the most destructive, mechanized land war since 1945, with attendant grievous loss of infrastructure, housing, and manpower; it will forever border Russia, the aggressor power in the war, still probably ruled by a repressive regime and still occupying or claiming Ukrainian territory; and a third or more of Ukraine's prewar population—disproportionately women and children—will begin the reconstruction period internally displaced or as refugees outside the country, mainly in other European countries. As a location for those allocating international assistance and in which private business would want to invest, Ukraine will also have to contend with its post-1991 record as the slowest-growing post-Soviet state with an unenviable record of corruption and state capture by oligarchs.[6]

---

[4] Derek W. Urwin, *The Community of Europe: A History of European Integration Since 1945*, 2nd ed., Routledge, 1995. The Warsaw Pact and Soviet Union states that joined the EU included Estonia, Latvia, Lithuania, Poland, Hungary, Czech Republic, Slovakia, Romania, and Bulgaria. With the incorporation of the German Democratic Republic (the former East Germany) in the Federal Republic of Germany (the former West Germany), the total is ten. Croatia and Slovenia also joined the EU, but they were part of now-former Yugoslavia and not in the Warsaw Pact.

[5] For convenience, in describing the reconstruction of Central and Eastern Europe after the Cold War, we use the term *European Union* or *EU* even for the period of 1989 to 1993.

[6] Helsinki Commission Staff, *The Internal Enemy: A Helsinki Commission Staff Report on Corruption in Ukraine,* Commission on Security and Cooperation in Europe, October 2017.

Security Requirements of a Post-War Settlement

Security and reconstruction are interdependent: Security fosters reconstruction, and reconstruction fosters security. In post-war environments, sustained improvement in the security situation must be achieved before many reconstruction efforts—such as the rebuilding of physical infrastructure, political reforms, democratization, economic revitalization, and the return of refugees and displaced persons—can take root.[7] Provisions for security are thus an essential component of any reconstruction plan.

The need to protect European states participating in the Marshall Plan and to enable them to take better advantage of it led to the creation of the North Atlantic Treaty Organization (NATO).[8] With the end of the Cold War, NATO expanded to provide this protection to the transforming nations of the former Warsaw Pact. NATO troops, in their capacity as peacekeepers, secured the settlements that ended the post-Yugoslav wars in the Western Balkans.[9]

The fact that Russia borders Ukraine to the north and east will not change, and Moscow's rulers likely will remain intent on undermining Ukraine's transformation into an independent and prosperous country. To the extent that Russia remains ruled by a repressive, irredentist regime, this reality will cast a long shadow over Ukraine's recovery and reconstruction. NATO membership for Ukraine would be one way to secure Ukraine's reconstruction by discouraging renewed Russian attacks, but the necessary unanimity among existing NATO members for such a step is not assured, and the prospect of Ukraine's admission to NATO could itself prove an obstacle to concluding the war, causing Russia to reject an otherwise acceptable settlement. In Chapter 7,

---

[7] Anga R. Timilsina and James Dobbins, "Shaping the Policy Priorities for Post-Conflict Reconstruction," *Policy Insight*, Vol. 1, No. 5, CP-521-(10/07), 2007, p. 1; Louay Constant, Shelly Culbertson, Jonathan S. Blake, Mary Kate Adgie, and Hardika Dayalani, *In Search of a Durable Solution: Examining the Factors Influencing Postconflict Refugee Returns*, RAND Corporation, RR-A1327-1, 2021.

[8] Melvyn P. Leffler, "The United States and the Strategic Dimensions of the Marshall Plan," *Diplomatic History*, Vol. 12, No. 3, Summer 1988. As Benn Steil notes, "an indispensable complementary factory in the success of [the Marshall Plan's] aid was credible U.S. security guarantees" (Benn Steil, "No Marshall Plan for Ukraine: Geography and Geopolitics Dictate a Different Reconstruction Model," *Foreign Affairs*, May 13, 2022).

[9] Dobbins et al., 2003, p. 87.

we examine several approaches to post-war security for Ukraine, recognizing that the choice will be influenced by how the war ends.

Given that reconstruction is an effort intimately connected with stable and enduring post-war security arrangements, it is necessary to consider a variety of futures: how the war between Russia and Ukraine may end, the nature of such a settlement, and how such a settlement can be secured. Avril Haines, the U.S. Director of National Intelligence, speaking in late June 2022, laid out three scenarios for the future trajectory of the war:

- **Russia ascendant.** Russian's continuing progress in eastern Ukraine might break Ukrainians' will to fight and allow the Russian military to take over even more of the country. Russia refocuses attacks on Kharkiv in the northeast or Odesa in the southwest.
- **Stalemate.** Russia dominates Ukraine's east but would not be able to go much farther. The conflict remains a grinding struggle in which Russia or Ukraine makes incremental gains but neither achieves a breakthrough. Russia secures Luhansk and much of Donetsk and consolidates its control in southern Ukraine.
- **Ukraine ascendant.** Ukraine halts Russia's advance in the east and succeeds in launching counterattacks. Ukraine further rolls back the front line in the Donbas and begins to make smaller gains, likely in Kherson or elsewhere in southern Ukraine.[10]

There are other ways the war might end, and in December 2022, little more than six months after this intelligence assessment, Russian progress in eastern Ukraine had stalled and Russian forces had been pushed back. As the war continues, one side or the other might achieve total victory, possibly accompanied by regime change for the loser. Liberalizing regime change in Russia could lead to a withdrawal from most or all of Ukraine. Or the war might not end at all but rather subside back into the sporadic fighting that occurred from 2014 until the launch of President Vladimir Putin's

---

[10] David Leonhardt, "Three War Scenarios," *New York Times*, July 6, 2022; Julian E. Barnes, "Putin Wants to Take Most of Ukraine, but a Quick Breakthrough Is Unlikely, the Top U.S. Intelligence Official Says," *New York Times*, June 29, 2022; Anton Troianovski and Julian E. Barnes, "Russian Invasion of Ukraine: 'The Work Is Going Smoothly': Putin Suggests That He Can Outlast Ukraine and the West," *New York Times*, June 30, 2022.

so-called special military operation. Or the war might expand, bringing in new belligerents or escalating beyond the conventional level.[11] It seems unlikely, however, that either side in this conflict can achieve all its aims on the battlefield or at the negotiating table, although these outcomes cannot be ruled out. Peace, when it comes, seems likely to take the form of a cease-fire or armistice that defers the permanent resolution of some territorial issues, leaving both sides dissatisfied. However, even such a peace will form the minimum conditions for reconstruction to start.

To endure, even an interim settlement must appear to both sides as preferable to renewed conflict. The military and economic costs of renewed conflict must outweigh any further benefits for both sides. If any settlement were to appear to be merely an operational pause to allow forces to regroup and reconstitute before the resumption of conventional conflict, there will be diminished support among donors and investors to rebuild what seems destined to be knocked down again.

Interim agreements that postpone rather than resolve territorial or political disputes can prove remarkably durable as long as they continue to reflect the underlying balance of power. The provisional division of Germany at the end of WWII lasted 45 years. The armistice that ended the fighting in Korea in 1953—in which the two parties agreed to disengagement, arms limitations, and monitoring measures—remains in force as of spring 2023, although the two Koreas continue to regard themselves formally as still at war. A China divided between two claimants from the end of its civil war in 1949 remains so. And a United Nations (UN) peacekeeping force has been patrolling the cease fire lines between Turkish- and Greek-speaking populations in Cyprus since the Turkish incursion of 1974.

Division did not prevent West Germany, South Korea, or the People's Republic of China from fashioning three of the 20th century's most successful states, or Germany, South Korea, Taiwan, and Cyprus from becoming firmly established democracies. Ukraine's reconstruction offers an opportunity to set Ukraine on a similar trajectory, even if it unfolds under an interim settlement rather than a conclusive end to the war.

---

[11] Bryan Frederick, Samuel Charap, Scott Boston, Stephen J. Flanagan, Michael J. Mazarr, Jennifer D. P. Moroney, and Karl P. Mueller, *Pathways to Russian Escalation Against NATO from the Ukraine War*, RAND Corporation, PE-A1971-1, 2022.

Methods and Goals

In this report, we examine past reconstruction events to draw lessons for the successful reconstruction of Ukraine. As of early 2023, much had already been written on this topic.[12] Our analysis seeks to add value by drawing lessons from the most-relevant, mostly European examples; drawing on disaster recovery approaches; and integrating reconstruction with security issues. To conduct this analysis, we reviewed the academic, official, and policy literature on reconstruction in Japan after WWII and Europe after WWII, the Cold War, and the wars in the Western Balkans. These reconstruction efforts all involved either advanced capitalist economies or European countries that would be integrated into the broader European project and were thus very unlike the cases of Afghanistan and Iraq, but very much like the challenge that Ukraine is facing. We also reviewed publicly available data on financing and economic performance in these cases. We then reviewed the literature on recovery and reconstruction from natural disasters, focusing on cases in which the United States led the recovery effort or those that occurred in advanced capitalist economies. For security, we reviewed the academic and policy literature on deterrence and post-war security arrangements. We also drew on the decades-long personal experience of our research team and the suggestions and experience of our formal

---

[12] Yuriy Gorodnichenko, Ilona Sologoub, and Beatrice Weder di Mauro, eds., *Rebuilding Ukraine: Principles and Policies*, Centre for Economic Policy Research, November 2022; Vladyslav Galushko, Iskra Kirova, Inna Pidluska, and Daniela Schwarzer, *War and Peace: Supporting Ukraine to Prevail, Rebuild, and Prosper*, Open Society Foundations, October 2022; Stephen Lewarne, Nell Todd, Joe Mariani, Joniel Sung-Jin Cha, and Stuart Williamson, "The Reconstruction of Ukraine: Historical Lessons for Postwar Reconstruction of Ukraine," Deloitte, October 10, 2022; Heather A. Conley, *A Modern Marshall Plan for Ukraine: Seven Lessons from History to Deliver Hope*, German Marshall Fund of the United States, October 3, 2022; Ronja Ganster, Jacob Kirkegaard, Thomas Kleine-Brockhoff, and Bruce Stokes, *Designing Ukraine's Recovery in the Spirit of the Marshall Plan: Principles, Architecture, Financing, Accountability: Recommendations for Donor Countries*, German Marshall Fund of the United States, September 2022; Mark Temnycky, "A Marshall Plan for Ukraine," Center for European Policy Analysis, May 25, 2022; Torbjörn Becker, Barry Eichengreen, Yuriy Gorodnichenko, Sergei Guriev, Simon Johnson, Tymofiy Mylovanov, Kenneth Rogoff, and Beatrice Weder di Mauro, eds., *A Blueprint for the Reconstruction of Ukraine*, Centre for Economic Policy Research Press, April 5, 2022.

and informal reviewers, all of whom either had senior positions in the U.S. government or international institutions involving post-war or natural disaster reconstruction or deep analytical experience in these topics.

Our findings are aimed first at informing U.S. policymakers who will need to determine U.S. interests and involvement in the reform and reconstruction of Ukraine. These findings also are intended to be useful to Ukrainians themselves as they create and revise their own reform and reconstruction plans and to Ukraine's European and other international partners, who will support its reform and reconstruction.

Structure of This Report

In Chapter 2, to draw lessons about what policies and actions might make for successful reconstruction, we review the record of post-war reconstruction efforts of developed societies emerging from conflict, beginning with those that occurred in Europe and Japan after WWII, the reform and recovery of former Warsaw Pact countries after the end of the Cold War, and the ongoing reform and recovery of the Western Balkan Six after the Yugoslav wars of the 1990s.[13] We then discuss lessons from post–natural disaster reconstruction in Chapter 3. Having looked at other examples, in Chapter 4, we discuss Ukraine's record since independence in 1991 and highlight that the country will not be engaging only in reconstruction, but in reforms to finally capture the benefits of emerging as a free country with the dissolution of the Soviet Union. In Chapter 5, we focus on how reform and reconstruction in Ukraine might be financed. In Chapter 6, we present principles for organizing international support for reform and reconstruction. In Chapter 7, we explore alternative approaches for post-war security arrangements that could help to enable reform and reconstruction. Finally, in Chapter 8, we draw on all chapters to present our conclusions with policy directions for supporting a secure and prosperous future for Ukraine.

---

[13] The Western Balkan Six countries are Albania, Bosnia and Herzegovina, Kosovo, Montenegro, North Macedonia, and Serbia.

CHAPTER 2

Historical Perspectives on Reconstruction

The economic and social damage caused by Russia's war on Ukraine has been enormous. A World Bank assessment, authored jointly with the European Commission and the Government of Ukraine, estimated that as of the beginning of June 2022, direct damage had amounted to more than $97 billion, and losses of production and other economic activities had amounted to $252 billion; the authors estimated recovery and reconstruction needs at $349 billion.[1] In September 2022, another analysis estimated total infrastructure damage at $127 billion.[2] The International Monetary Fund (IMF) has estimated that the war will have led to a 35 percent decline in Ukraine's gross domestic product (GDP) in 2022 relative to 2021.[3] This is greater than the 26 percent peak-to-trough GDP decline that the United States experienced from 1929 to 1933 during the Great Depression, and it is worse than most of the greatest economic disasters of the 20th century.[4]

---

[1] World Bank, Government of Ukraine, and the European Commission, *Ukraine: Rapid Damage and Needs Assessment*, July 31, 2022, p. 11.

[2] KSE Institute, Ministry of Community Development and Territories of Ukraine, Ministry of Infrastructure of Ukraine, and Ministry of Health of Ukraine, *Assessment of Damages in Ukraine Due to Russia's Military Aggression as of September 1, 2022*, September 2022, p. 3.

[3] International Monetary Fund, *World Economic Outlook: Countering the Cost-of-Living Crisis*, October 2022a, p. 42.

[4] U.S. GDP data is from the U.S. Bureau of Economic Analysis, "Current-Dollar and 'Real' Gross Domestic Product," spreadsheet, October 27, 2022a. The historical record on economic disasters can be found in Robert J. Barro, "Rare Disasters and Asset Markets in the Twentieth Century," *Quarterly Journal of Economics*, Vol. 121, No. 3, August

Eventually, Ukraine and its global partners will face the challenge of reconstruction. For this, they can draw on historical precedent. Allied powers faced an analogous challenge with a destroyed Japan and Europe after WWII. Less than half a century later, in the early 1990s, the challenge was the reconstitution of Central and Eastern Europe, newly freed from the Soviet orbit. Although this did not involve wartime destruction, it did involve completely reshaping governments and economic systems and dealing with often-obsolete economic infrastructure. Shortly thereafter came the challenge of reconstructing the Western Balkans from the ruins of the former Yugoslavia. Beyond these examples, there are parallels to be drawn from the aftermaths of natural disasters, such as hurricanes, floods, or earthquakes. Such disasters can cause enormous levels of infrastructure damage as well as damage to social and economic systems. This chapter focuses on the events following WWII, the reconstitution of Central and Eastern Europe, and the reconstruction of the Western Balkans.[5] Chapter 3 provides more details about post-disaster reconstruction.

Japan After World War II

When WWII ended, Japan was a ruined economy. Gross national product in 1945 was only about 60 percent of the average from 1934 to 1936.[6] The allied

---

2006. Barro defines an *economic disaster* as a decline of real per capita GDP by 15 percent or greater. Most of these disasters were related to World War I, WWII, or the Great Depression.

[5] We do not examine lessons from more-recent U.S.-supported reconstruction efforts in Afghanistan and Iraq for two reasons: (1) These countries were seeking to rebuild in the midst of ongoing civil wars and insurgencies (which Ukraine is not experiencing), and (2) unlike Iraq and Afghanistan, Ukraine, for all its challenges, is a semi-developed country in Europe with a long-established industrial base, educated populace, and internationally competitive farm sector.

[6] Koichi Hamada and Munehisa Kasuya, "The Reconstruction and Stabilization of the Postwar Japanese Economy: Possible Lessons for Eastern Europe," Center Discussion Paper No. 672, Economic Growth Center, Yale University, 1992. National and global statistical authorities originally reported measures of national income in terms of gross national product, or GNP. Reporting eventually shifted to gross domestic product, or GDP. In the United States, this occurred in 1991 (Kelly Ramey, "The Changeover from

strategic bombing campaign destroyed almost half of all structures in the 66 cities that it targeted, amounting to 2.2 million buildings.[7] In 1946, the year after surrender, Japan experienced very high inflation: The retail price index rose 6.1 times (not 6.1 percent), an underestimation of true inflation because it excluded black-market prices.[8] The country was not in control of its own policy, but rather under the control of the Supreme Commander of Allied Powers (SCAP) (also known as the General Headquarters), although the SCAP was working through the reconstituted government of Japan.

SCAP instituted three early reforms that aimed to demilitarize and democratize Japan but that also served to help restore its economy.[9] These were (1) land reform, (2) breaking up the conglomerates known as the *zaibatsu*, and (3) labor reform. Land reform resulted in the transfer of 81 percent of all tenant land to tenant farmers, resulting in better work incentives for these farmers and an accompanying leap in agricultural productivity. The breakup of the zaibatsu created a better competitive environment and brought in new management. Labor reforms resulted in new legislation to improve working conditions and the rapid growth of unionization.

As part of its efforts to restore growth, Japan created a Priority Production System that financed certain industrial sectors through the issuance of government bonds but that effectively funded investment by printing money.[10] From a low in 1946, industrial production grew 2.7 times through

---

GNP to GDP: A Milestone in BEA History," *Survey of Current Business*, Vol. 101, No. 3, March 2021). GNP, now called gross national income, measures the income received by all nationals of a specific country, no matter where they are located, while GDP measures all production within a specific country or territory ("Gross Domestic Product as a Measure of U.S. Production," *Survey of Current Business*, Vol. 71, No. 8, August 1991, p. 8). For many countries, especially large economies, the two measures are often very close.

[7] Donald R. Davis and David E. Weinstein, "Bombs, Bones, and Break Points: The Geography of Economic Activity," *American Economic Review*, Vol. 92, No. 5, December 2002.

[8] Yoshio Suzuki, "Difficulties and Challenges: Japan's Post-War History of Economic Trends and Monetary Policy," Center on Japanese Economy and Business, Columbia Business School, Working Paper Series No. 360, August 2017.

[9] This paragraph draws from Hamada and Kasuya, 1992.

[10] Hamada and Kasuya, 1992, p. 11.

1950.[11] But this method of financing accelerated inflation, especially through early 1948. To combat runaway inflation, occupation authorities brought in a commercial bank president from Detroit named Joseph Dodge (who had previously headed the fiscal department of the U.S. military government in Germany).

The resulting stabilization plan had nine points, the first four of which were designed to counter inflation and included instructions to balance the budget, increase tax collection, cut back on lending, and stabilize wages (the other five points were not pursued). The balanced-budget provision became known as the *Dodge Line*. Results were dramatic: Black market prices fell, the household savings rate rose, and the government was better able to ease up on price controls. At the same time, economic activity slowed.[12] Japanese real gross national product grew by 8.6 percent in fiscal year 1947 and 12.7 percent in fiscal year 1948, but it slowed to 2.1 percent in fiscal year 1949.[13]

The tight fiscal policy might have led to a longer-term slump, except that the Korean War started. The conflict expanded worldwide demand, and U.S. troop spending in Japan particularly expanded economic activity there, leading to rapid growth for several years. In retrospect, the stabilization plan of 1949 was "needed to bring the postwar economy to a stable growth path with price stability, business confidence, and capital accumulation," and it put the Japanese economy in an ideal position to benefit from the Korean War boom.[14]

Throughout the occupation, U.S. actions included assistance, although these were not substantial transfers in relation to the size of Japan's economy. Between 1946 and 1952, U.S. assistance totaled $2.2 billion (about $21.3 billion in 2021 dollars), of which $1.7 billion ($16.5 billion in 2021 dollars) were grants and the rest loans.[15] Most of the funding was distributed through two

---

[11] Jerome B. Cohen, "Table IV-2, Indexes of Japanese Industrial Production, 1946, 1948, 1950–1956," in *Japan's Postwar Economy*, Indiana University Press, 1958.

[12] Hamada and Kasuya, 1992, pp. 21–23.

[13] Hamada and Kasuya, 1992, p. 47.

[14] Hamada and Kasuya, 1992, p. 24.

[15] Nina Serafino, Curt Tarnoff, and Dick K. Nanto, *U.S. Occupation Assistance: Iraq, Germany, and Japan Compared*, Congressional Research Service, RL33331, March 23, 2006. This source provided values in current dollars and in 2005 dollars. To convert to

programs: Government Relief in Occupied Areas and Economic Rehabilitation in Occupied Areas.[16] The $2.2 billion amounted to 5 percent of cumula-
tive nominal Japanese national income from 1949 to 1952.[17]

Japan's true era of rapid growth started after 1958 and continued through
the end of the 1960s. For example, in the three-year period of fiscal years
1955 to 1958, growth of real GDP (called gross domestic expenditure in the
data) averaged 7.1 percent annually. For every subsequent three-year period
through 1971, it averaged more than 8 percent, and in five of those 13 three-
year periods, there was an average double-digit percentage increase.[18]

Although the 1960s were well past the period of immediate post-war
reconstruction, an examination of this rapid growth may provide useful
information for Ukraine reconstruction.[19] To strengthen a fading U.S.-Japan
security alliance, the two countries started negotiations on a new security
treaty, concluded in 1960 (although with significant contention among the
Japanese population). At the same time, the United States (1) arranged a
large amount of low-interest loans to Japan via the World Bank, the U.S.
Export-Import Bank, and U.S. commercial banks; (2) approved a reduction
in Japanese defense spending, freeing up money for the civilian economy;

2021 dollars, we followed U.S. Census Bureau methods and data as described in U.S.
Census Bureau, "Current Versus Constant (or Real) Dollars," webpage, last revised September 12, 2022.

[16] Haruhiko Fukui, "Economic Planning in Postwar Japan: A Case Study in Policy
Making," *Asian Survey*, Vol. 12, No. 4, April 1972.

[17] Japanese national income data are from United Nations, *Statistical Yearbook 1956*,
No. 8, Statistical Office of the United Nations, Department of Economic and Social
Affairs, 1956, p. 470. The yearbook gives values in yen amounts, and we converted these
at 360 yen to the dollar, the official rate that took effect April 25, 1949 ("Japanese Yen
Pegged at Rate of 360 for $1," *New York Times*, April 23, 1949). Note that we are com-
paring assistance between 1946 and 1952 with cumulative GDP between 1949 and 1952
because of data limitations. Were we to compare assistance between 1946 and 1952 with
cumulative GDP between 1946 and 1952, the ratio of assistance to GDP would be lower
than 5 percent.

[18] Cabinet Office of Japan, "Gross Domestic Expenditure at Constant Prices (Fiscal
Year)," Economic and Social Research Institute, webpage, undated.

[19] This discussion draws from Michael Beckley, Yusaku Horiuchi, and Jennifer M.
Miller, "America's Role in the Making of Japan's Economic Miracle," *Journal of East
Asian Studies*, Vol. 18, 2018, pp. 4–6.

and (3) helped promote Japanese exports to the United States, a policy that continued throughout the 1960s. Thus, in Japan, the security treaty provided stability and fiscal scope for domestic investment, international borrowing provided additional capital, and the United States provided export markets, all of which combined to stimulate sustained economic growth.

Western Europe After World War II

The Marshall Plan to help Europe after WWII is probably the most heralded reconstruction plan in modern history. It laid the foundations for two decades of economic growth, twice as fast as in any 20-year period before or since.[20] It has inspired numerous analysts and policymakers to approach Ukraine's reconstruction by calling for a "new Marshall Plan" or to use the Marshall Plan as a framing to consider how a realistic plan for Ukraine's reconstruction could be designed.[21]

The Marshall Plan, formally the European Recovery Program, is often described as the aid program that delivered necessary capital to Western Europe to pay for reconstruction. But U.S. funding was relatively limited, and in some respects, Europe was already rebuilding. Instead, although the money was useful to reconstruction, its effect on fostering good policy was likely far more important. And even with significant funding and good policy, the U.S. security umbrella that came with NATO shortly thereafter might well have been the decisive factor to ensure that Europe achieved successful reconstruction and sustained economic growth.

The Marshall Plan began in 1948, years after other efforts to reconstruct Europe were already underway. Established in November 1943 and lasting through March 1949, the United Nations Relief and Rehabilitation Administration (UNRRA) distributed large amounts of aid in kind and in cash to a recovering Europe. Backed by 52 governments as well as private orga-

---

[20] De Long and Eichengreen, 1991, pp. 50–51.

[21] Conley, 2022; Temnycky, 2022; Andrey Kortunov, "Is a Marshall Plan for Ukraine Possible?" Russian International Affairs Council, November 3, 2022.

nizations and individuals, and active in 16 countries, UNRRA distributed almost $1 billion in commodities and almost $2 billion in direct relief.[22]

The United States supported other aid programs to Europe as well. As Paris was liberated in August 1944, the United States concluded a Lend-Lease agreement with the liberated French government, resulting in $400 billion worth of consumer and industrial goods. An "Eight Months Program" to supply France from November 1944 to June 1945 was subsequently approved in November 1944, followed by an import program agreed to in 1945. The latter two plans supplied almost $2.6 billion worth of food, raw materials, and industrial goods.[23] Likewise, in Germany, under the category of Government and Relief in Occupied Areas, the United States disbursed grants worth $490.5 million in 1946 and 1947 ($5.2 billion in 2021 dollars).[24] By one estimate, total U.S. aid to Europe from 1945 to 1947 was almost $13 billion in then-current dollars ($138.3 billion in 2021 dollars), about the same as the subsequent Marshall Plan.[25]

By 1947, however, it was apparent that Europe was still struggling. The idea for a new relief plan actually came from the military, intent on strengthening Europe so that U.S. troops could withdraw.[26] Secretary of State George C. Marshall introduced the idea in a commencement address at Harvard University on June 5, 1947, and worked closely with Republican Senator Arthur Vandenberg to get the necessary legislation through Con-

---

[22] "United Nations Rehabilitation and Relief Administration," *International Organization*, Vol. 3, No. 3, August 1949, p. 568.

[23] John S. Hill, "American Efforts to Aid French Reconstruction Between Lend-Lease and the Marshall Plan," *Journal of Modern History*, Vol. 64, No. 3, September 1992.

[24] Serafino, Tarnoff, and Nanto, 2006. This source provided values in current dollars and in 2005 dollars. To convert to 2021 dollars, we followed U.S. Census Bureau methods and data as described in U.S. Census Bureau, 2022.

[25] Council on Foreign Relations, "'The Marshall Plan: Dawn of the Cold War,' by Benn Steil," webpage, February 13, 2018. This source provided the value in current dollars. To convert to 2021 dollars, we followed U.S. Census Bureau methods and data as described in U.S. Census Bureau, 2022.

[26] Council on Foreign Relations, 2018.

gress.[27] Despite some opposition, with Vandenberg's help, support for the legislation was bipartisan.

The plan ran from April 1948 through June 1952, although nearly all the $13.2 billion dollars ($127.9 billion in 2018 dollars) had been made available by June 1951.[28] This total amounted to about 1.4 percent of U.S. GDP, and 2.6 percent of the GDP of the 16 recipient countries.[29] The plan was run by a U.S. agency called the Economic Cooperation Administration, led by Paul G. Hoffman, previously the president of Studebaker Corporation (an auto manufacturer).

The Marshall Plan had three goals: (1) expand European agriculture and industrial production; (2) restore currencies, budgets, and public finances; and (3) foster international trade.[30] Recipient countries had to agree on a plan of action. Presciently, the United States required that the European recipient countries develop cooperative approaches to recovery, coordinated through a purpose-built regional organization, the Organisation for European Economic Co-operation (OEEC).[31] An initial conference of the Euro-

---

[27] Curt Tarnoff, *The Marshall Plan: Design, Accomplishments, and Significance*, Congressional Research Service, R45079, January 18, 2018.

[28] Benn Steil and Benjamin Della Rocca, "It Takes More Than Money to Make a Marshall Plan," *Geo-Graphics* blog, Council on Foreign Relations, April 9, 2018. This source provided the value in current dollars and 2018 dollars. To convert to 2021 dollars, we followed U.S. Census Bureau methods and data as described in U.S. Census Bureau, 2022. Note that the 2018 dollar value listed in the source was $135 billion, above our 2021 dollar value. Reasons for the discrepancy are not clear. We used the consumer price index to make the conversion, the same method used by the U.S. Census Bureau. We also used the GDP deflator and calculated a value of $116.7 billion in 2021 dollars (U.S. Bureau of Economic Analysis, "National Income and Product Accounts: Table 1.1.9. Implicit Price Deflators for Gross Domestic Product," interactive data file, last revised on December 22, 2022b).

[29] For the 1.4 percent, Marshall Plan expenditures are from Tarnoff, 2018. U.S. GDP figures are from U.S. Bureau of Economic Analysis, 2022a. The 2.6 percent figure is from SALT, "Benn Steil: 'The Marshall Plan: Dawn of the Cold War,' SALT Talks 137," webpage, January 11, 2021.

[30] Tarnoff, 2018, p. 1.

[31] The OEEC later transformed itself in the Organisation for Economic Co-operation and Development (OECD) which continues as a leading organization in promoting economic growth and cooperation among developed and threshold countries.

pean countries before the introduction of the Marshall Plan, taking place as the Committee of European Economic Cooperation, created a draft proposal for the design of the program. However, the proposal had significant differences among countries regarding trade liberalization and levels of state control of the economy. The U.S. Department of State responded with conditions—including more-specific commitments and greater responsibility for meeting common objectives—that were included in the final report of the European countries in September 1947.[32]

There were three main economic or socio-economic reasons why the Marshall Plan worked.[33] First, it contributed to stabilization. European economies in 1948 were suffering from high inflation and the policy response of price controls, leading to distorted and suppressed production. Marshall Plan funding gave governments the room to balance budgets—necessary for inflation to be stopped—and for controls to be removed without demanding excessive sacrifices of the population. Conditionality was part of this program. Marshall Plan recipients had to provide matching funds, and those funds could be used only with permission of the U.S. government, which provided permission only if there were a stabilization program. This conditionality also slowed down any impulses toward nationalization.

Second, conditionality required that policies allow market forces to operate, at least to some degree. This included realistic exchange rates, encouragement of exports, and European integration through the removal of quotas and trade controls to foster market competition. Finally, the Marshall Plan enabled labor peace while it operated, and this might have carried over into two decades of European growth during which the labor supply expanded to match labor demand and wages rose *with* productivity increases rather than *above* them. Among the four major economies of Germany, France, Italy, and the United Kingdom, the United States had the most influence on conditionalities in Germany, which grew the fastest, and the least in the United Kingdom, which grew the slowest.[34]

---

[32] Tarnoff, 2018, pp. 3–4.

[33] De Long and Eichengreen, 1991, pp. 43–55.

[34] De Long and Eichengreen, 1991, p. 55.

But there was another reason for the plan's success beyond economics. At the same time that the Marshall Plan started, the United States extended a security guarantee to Europe through NATO.[35] This proved essential to encouraging business investment and longer-term economic policy in Europe. In fact, the United States occasionally let economic conditionality slide for political purposes: The United States let France and Italy go their own ways on some policies as long as they kept Communists out of their governments, which they did. Even at the time, security was viewed as an essential component of reconstruction. U.S. Department of State officials "called NATO a military ERP, European Recovery Plan."[36]

Any discussion about the success of the Marshall Plan would be remiss to exclude the roles that public and congressional support played. As a report from 1947—the time the plan was being developed—noted, "the executive branch can suggest, but it will be for Congress to decide whether or not further aid shall be granted to Europe and on what terms."[37] Support for the plan was far from guaranteed, with an American public weary from the economic sacrifices of WWII, a Democratic president facing a Republican Congress, and members of Congress publicly decrying the plan as "a socialist blueprint" and "money down a rat hole."[38] The Truman administration undertook a massive, grassroots public education campaign to gain the support of the American people. The administration also included members of Congress in the development of the legislation from the beginning, and it set up committees to provide Congress with details on the plan's implementation and positive impact. These efforts were critical to secure buy-in for a program that would cost American taxpayers more than $13 billion.[39]

---

[35] Benn Steil, "Why It Is So Hard to Repeat the Marshall Plan," German Marshall Fund of the United States, June 6, 2022.

[36] Council on Foreign Relations, 2018.

[37] F. Van Schaick, "Conditions for American Aid," *Congressional Quarterly Editorial Research Reports*, Vol. 2, October 17, 1947.

[38] Tarnoff, 2018, p. 5.

[39] Tarnoff, 2018, pp. 5–6.

Central and Eastern Europe in the 1990s

In some ways, the challenges faced by the countries of Central and Eastern Europe in 1989 and those of the former Soviet Union at the end of 1991 were very different from the challenges Ukraine faces in 2023. Along with many other problems, the countries of Central and Eastern Europe and the former Soviet Union had to shift from a communist command economy to a market economy. Ukraine was among those countries and made the shift, although not in a way that spurred rapid economic growth.[40]

In some ways, however, the challenges were similar. The reforming countries had obsolete industrial plants and economies that needed to be transformed. Ukraine in 2023 has a functioning economy, but one that needs to be transformed to have modern plants and equipment and a modern industrial structure. And Ukraine is still struggling with some of its legacies from the Soviet Union, including a large share of state-owned enterprises in the economy and high levels of corruption.

Reforms in Eastern Europe started in 1989, when those countries broke free of the Soviet orbit. But they were beset with economic crises, including high or hyper-inflation, empty store shelves, high budget deficits, and severe output declines. In fact, system disintegration called for rapid reforms.[41] The then–finance minister of Poland, Leszek Balcerowicz, identified the major elements of reform that his country needed. These were also reforms needed throughout the region. These elements included

- macroeconomic stabilization: bringing down inflation, balancing budgets, decontrolling prices, and ending shortages
- economic liberalization: reforming market institutions, such as by modernizing commercial law and opening closed markets to international trade, especially to and from the EU

---

[40] Pekka Sutela, *The Underachiever: Ukraine's Economy Since 1991*, Carnegie Endowment for International Peace, March 2012; Mykhailo Minakov, "Three Decades of Ukraine's Independence," *Focus Ukraine* blog, Kennan Institute, September 13, 2021.

[41] World Bank, *From Plan to Market: World Development Report 1996*, Oxford University Press, 1996, p. 11.

- privatization: moving state assets into private hands where they could be operated more efficiently.[42]

For industrial restructuring, hard budget constraints needed to be instituted throughout the region, meaning that firms needed to survive without government subsidies or otherwise be sold or liquidated.[43] The subsidies were one factor in spurring inflation, as they had been in Japan before the Dodge Line was instituted. Part of this restructuring needed to involve new legal and regulatory institutions.

Balcerowicz's stabilization plan provides one illustration of how reforms were carried out quickly and effectively. On January 1, 1990, price controls were ended, the exchange rate was devalued, and the Polish currency was made convertible. All of this was backstopped by balance of payments loans from the IMF to shore up Poland's foreign exchange reserves and by a $1 billion stabilization fund put together by the Group of Seven (G7) leading industrial countries.[44] Inflation jumped during January 1990 but then leveled off, and goods started returning to store shelves.

Aside from the stabilization, Poland passed new legislation to introduce market institutions. Notably, although the reforms were quick, they were not necessarily radical. Poland specifically did not want to create all new institutions. Rather, it wanted to model its institutions on those that already existed in Western Europe because those institutions had a proven record of working.[45]

Successful reforms in Central and Eastern Europe had significant external support. Certainly, there was financial support. This included financing

---

[42] Jeffrey Sachs, "Progress of Economic Reform in Eastern Europe," presentation, College of Saint Benedict and Saint John's University, Clemens Lecture Series No. 5, October 3, 1991.

[43] World Bank, *Transition: The First Ten Years: Analysis and Lessons for Eastern Europe and the Former Soviet Union*, 2002, pp. xvii–xviii.

[44] Sachs, 1991; Jeffrey Sachs and David Lipton, "Poland's Economic Reform," *Foreign Affairs*, Vol. 69, No. 3, Summer 1990. The G7 comprises Canada, France, Germany, Italy, Japan, the United Kingdom, and United States, along with the EU as a so-called nonenumerated member.

[45] Jeffrey Sachs, "Shock Therapy in Poland: Perspectives of Five Years," presentation, University of Utah, Tanner Lectures on Human Values, April 7, 1994.

from multilateral institutions and official bilateral creditors, as well as debt relief.[46] But financial support also included conditionality and expectations that political reforms would move in a democratic direction. The European Bank for Reconstruction and Development (EBRD)—which had been conceived in October 1989 and began operating in April 1991—was a new institution created to spur market-oriented reforms and promote the private sector.[47] Notably, and unlike other international financial institutions, the EBRD had a political mandate to support democracy, so it did not maintain political neutrality regarding the countries to which it lent, and its aim was specifically to support the private sector.[48] As of 2023, the EBRD had 71 shareholding countries along with the EU and the European Investment Bank and 35 portfolio countries receiving financing and advising services. Notably, the United States was the largest single shareholder, with 10 percent of the bank's capital; this illustrates U.S. involvement in recovery and reconstruction worldwide.[49] Other institutional innovation occurred, including the creation by the United States of enterprise funds, which we discuss in Chapter 5.

One other element was important to the reforms in Central and Eastern Europe. Just as greater levels of trade in post-WWII Europe (encouraged by the Marshall Plan) and increased exports by Japan (encouraged by the United States) helped those countries recover and grow, integration with Western Europe proved beneficial to post-communist Central and Eastern Europe. This was true not just economically but institutionally. A driving force behind this was the signing of formal European Association Agreements, which became better known as the Europe Agreements, between

---

[46] James Roaf, Ruben Atoyan, Bikas Joshi, and Krzysztof Krogulsi, *25 Years of Transition: Post-Communist Europe and the IMF*, International Monetary Fund, Regional Economic Issues Special Report, October 2014.

[47] European Bank for Reconstruction and Development, "The History of the EBRD," webpage, undated.

[48] Martin A. Weiss, *European Bank for Reconstruction and Development (EBRD)*, IF11419, Congressional Research Service, updated June 21, 2022.

[49] Weiss, 2022.

the EU and the newly freed countries.[50] The Europe Agreements liberalized access to EU markets and obligated the Central and Eastern European signatories to reform a wide variety of policies and institutions to bring them into alignment with EU policies and institutions, all with an eye toward eventual EU membership. Czechoslovakia, Hungary, and Poland were the first signatories in 1991, followed by Bulgaria, Romania, Estonia, Latvia, Lithuania, and Slovenia, all of which later became EU members.[51]

Linking to the EU led to sizable amounts of foreign direct investment from EU members as well as trade with those members. Taking only the early signatories—Czechoslovakia (later splitting into the Czech Republic and Slovakia), Hungary, and Poland, trade in goods with the then-12 members of the EU grew by 194 percent from 1989 to 1994, whereas trade with the rest of the world grew by 54 percent. In the subsequent five-year period from 1994 to 1999, trade in goods with the EU grew by 129 percent, whereas trade with the rest of the world grew by 91 percent.[52]

Reflective of this mix of economics and institutions, in 2014, the then–deputy managing director of the IMF, David Lipton, identified four factors in the successful transition, among which was "Magnet Europe":

> After years of isolation from the Western economic system, and after the distortions and deprivations of the communist system, most citizens just wanted to live in a normal country with a normal economy, and, given their history and geography, that vision was captured in the allure of reintegrating with Western Europe. The historic offer from the European Union to countries in the region provided a gravitational pull that helped policymakers justify and implement difficult reform steps.[53]

---

[50] Bartlomiej Kaminski, "The Europe Agreements and Transition: Unique Returns from Integrating into the European Union," in Sorin Antohi and Vladimir Tisaneaunu, eds., *Between Past and Future: The Revolutions of 1989 and Their Aftermath*, Central European University Press, 2000.

[51] Anthony Teasdale and Timothy Bainbridge, "Europe Agreement," *Penguin Companion to European Union*, webpage, September 2012.

[52] Trade data are drawn from UN, "UN Comtrade Database," undated.

[53] Roaf et al., 2014, pp. ix–x.

Through 2012, the majority of external funding had come from the EU. And in the five Central European countries of Czech Republic, Hungary, Poland, Slovakia, and Slovenia, more than half of external financing was in the form of foreign direct investment.[54] These countries also became linked to German supply chains, boosting export opportunities not only to the rest of Europe but to Asia. Ensuring that markets are available to Ukrainian producers will be relevant to its success as countries assist it with post-war reforms.

The Western Balkans

The final chapter of the end of the Soviet empire occurred in Yugoslavia and the Western Balkans in the 1990s. A brief armed confrontation between Slovenia and Yugoslavia, which resulted in Slovenia's independence in 1991 (with Germany's crucial support), started the breakup of Yugoslavia, followed by war between Croatia and Serbia and then the independence war of Bosnia and Herzegovina, settled in the Dayton Accords of 1995.[55] The final act came in Kosovo in 1998–1999, which resulted in the first armed intervention by NATO.[56]

Recovery and reconstruction differed among the Western Balkan countries, depending in part on their levels of development and the nature of the support that they received from the EU. Slovenia, the most developed of the former Yugoslav republics, was soon accepted with Germany's support as an EU accession candidate country, and it entered the EU as a member in 2004.

Reconstruction focused on the so-called Western Balkan Six: Albania, Bosnia and Herzegovina, Kosovo, Montenegro, North Macedonia, and Ser-

---

[54] Roaf et al., 2014, p. 34.

[55] Dobbins et al., 2003, pp. 87–88.

[56] Richard Zink, "The EU and Reconstruction in the Western Balkans," in Jean Dufourcq and David S. Yost, eds., *NATO-EU Cooperation in Post Conflict Reconstruction*, NATO Defense College, Academic Research Branch, NDC Occasional Paper 15, May 2006.

bia.[57] These efforts have been decidedly less successful than those in Central and Eastern Europe in stimulating growth and democratization. They were also different from other efforts in that the successive conflicts in Slovenia, Croatia, Bosnia, Kosovo, and North Macedonia were fought among ethnic factions that had long shared a single state. These countries needed peacemaking first, then economic reform and institutional change in an environment in which incomes were far lower than in the rest of Europe. Also, the new countries were small, and their economies were poorly connected with external markets.

For most of the past 20 years, the EU has held primary responsibility for reconstruction. In some cases, action originated from within Europe. Italy took leadership in Albania under Operation Alba when that country nearly fell apart as a result of economic collapse from a series of pyramid schemes.[58] In other cases, for example in Kosovo, the EU had to be pushed:

> Not a week passed without Madeleine Albright (then American Secretary of State) or her Balkans frontman, Jim Dobbins, telephoning to find out how we were translating promises into contracts, plans and real-time spending. Our past performance did not give them much confidence.
>
> —Former EU External Relations Commissioner Chris Patten[59]

---

[57] Wouter Zweers, Giulia Cretti, Myrthe de Bon, Alban Dafa, Strahinja Subotić, Milena Muk, Arber Fetahu, Ardita Abazi Imeri, Emina Kuhinja, and Hata Kujraković, *The EU as a Promoter of Democracy or 'Stabilitocracy' in the Western Balkans?* Clingendael Institute and the Think for Europe Network, February 2022.

[58] James Dobbins, Seth G. Jones, Keith Crane, Christopher S. Chivvis, Andrew Radin, F. Stephen Larrabee, Nora Bensahel, Brooke K. Stearns, and Benjamin W. Goldsmith, *Europe's Role in Nation-Building: From the Balkans to the Congo*, RAND Corporation, MG-722-RC, 2008, pp. 7–8.

[59] The quotation appears in Chris Patten's memoir, *Not Quite the Diplomat: Home Truths About World Affairs*, Allen Lane, 2005, p. 166, as cited in Zink, 2006, p. 42. The quotation continues:

> This was the first big test of our ability to run things competently, and we passed it—speeding up delivery by cutting corners where we could, setting up the European Agency for Reconstruction, and giving the excellent officials sent out to manage it delegated authority and political cover.

Nonetheless, Europe recognized that it would have primary responsibility for the reconstruction and integration of the region, and in June 1999 announced a Stability Pact.[60] This was followed by the 2003 formal start of a process of accession to the EU.[61]

At the start of reconstruction efforts, each country in the region faced many challenges.[62] These included macroeconomic imbalances in the form of high trade and current account deficits, high unemployment, and high fiscal deficits. There were sectoral challenges, including deindustrialization, poorly functioning banking systems, poorly functioning state-owned enterprises that needed to be privatized, and institutional challenges, such as the lack of protection for private property, nonexistent contract enforcement, and the lack of the rule of law.

Each of the Western Balkan Six received assistance from the EU, the World Bank, the IMF, and the EBRD. The EU started the European Agency for Reconstruction in Kosovo in early 2000, and its work then spread to Serbia and Montenegro and to what is now known as North Macedonia. The EU's initial actions were more of an emergency nature, but then it engaged in repairing and building infrastructure, including connecting these countries to road networks, electricity grids, and gas systems.[63]

In Bosnia and Herzegovina, the EU started taking over nation-building leadership from the United States as early as 2002, when Paddy Ashdown became both the UN High Representative and the EU Special Representative. This expanded in 2004, when EUFOR (the EU Force in Bosnia and Herzegovina) and the EU military operation took over responsibility from NATO for enforcing the security provisions of the Dayton Accords.[64] Starting in 2002, the EU steered Bosnia and Herzegovina toward policies that would enable it to join the EU. The EU role continued to expand, while that

---

[60] Vladimir Gligorov, Mary Kaldor, and Loukas Tsoukalis, *Balkan Reconstruction and European Integration*, Hellenic Observatory, Centre for the Study of Global Governance, and Vienna Institute for International Economic Studies, October 1999.

[61] Zweers et al., 2022, p. 10.

[62] This draws from Gligorov, Kaldor, and Tsoukalis, 1999, pp. 13–16.

[63] Zink, 2006, p. 43.

[64] Dobbins et al., 2008, p. 139.

of other international institutions initially set up to help with Bosnia reconstruction, such as the 55-country Peace Implementation Council, receded.

All told, the economic track record of the Western Balkan Six has not been bad. Growth has been above that of the EU and the world as a whole, although the Western Balkan Six are all small, poor countries and so would be expected to growth faster. More-valid comparison countries would be Slovenia and the Eastern Balkan countries of Bulgaria and Romania, and most Western Balkan countries have grown in line with these countries.[65]

Despite this, reconstruction and EU accession negotiations have gone slowly. The reasons likely are complicated, and many may result from problems internal to each country and politics within the EU. Some certainly are related to the way the EU sought to influence the reform and accession process. Among these are ill-defined definitions of rule of law and therefore uncertainty over what constitutes compliance with EU conditionality, the exercise of vetoes by individual member countries that have blocked the EU's ability to reward progress or withhold benefits when countries backslide, and a lack of clear timetables.[66] The attractive power of joining the EU has not been enough to overcome misaligned incentives within the Western Balkan Six that have led their reforms to stall.

Despite these problems, each of these reconstruction efforts in the Western Balkan Six succeeded in consolidating the peace, rebuilding the economies, and introducing or strengthening democratic governance within the recipient societies. Ukraine and those who are preparing to help it rebuild have a rich legacy to draw on and good reason to aim for a transformative result.

---

[65] These comparisons are based on GDP data drawn from World Bank, "World Development Indicators," database, undated. The variable used is "GDP per capita (constant 2015 US$)," series code NY.GDP.PCAP.KD.

[66] Zweers et al., 2022. The report lists eight reasons in total and provides recommendations on next steps.

Conclusion

The United States, Europe, and the world have faced several major postwar reconstruction episodes that provide examples for how to proceed with Ukraine. Every situation will be different and demand its own tailored response. But several consistent patterns emerge that might be applicable to Ukraine's situation.

The initial post-conflict or transition period generally calls for humanitarian assistance because both the economy and government services are broken. Target countries have struggled for several years. Getting actual reconstruction or restructuring started can take time, sometimes years. Countries going through the post-conflict or transition period often face bouts of high inflation, and strong stabilization policies are needed and must be sequenced. Aid can help, but aid packages pale in comparison to actual investment expenditures. Rather, official assistance provides the opportunity to solve specific problems or create conditionalities that encourage good reconstruction policies. Furthermore, at least some financing needs to come from the country undergoing reconstruction—aid alone is likely to do little.

Reliance on market mechanisms has delivered success in multiple cases: These mechanisms are sometimes encouraged by aid packages. These market mechanisms are not just related to the domestic economy. Establishing international trade links, both through domestic economic reforms and the receptivity of trading partners—such as via trade agreements—proved essential in every case. Likewise, attracting foreign direct investment, again through domestic reforms and as a byproduct of international economic agreements, boosted reconstruction.

Finally, although reconstruction takes place in the socio-economic and governmental spheres, security provides a base on which all activity takes place. In every case, the strength of external security agreements has played a role in the strength of reconstruction, giving businesses and investors the confidence to take risks and make long-term economic commitments. We discuss security arrangements for Ukraine in Chapter 7.

CHAPTER 3

Lessons from Post–Natural Disaster Reconstruction Efforts

Russia's invasion of Ukraine has led to the destruction of infrastructure, disruption of public services, and damage to the social fabric in ways that have some similarities to destruction caused by natural hazards, such as fires, earthquakes, tsunamis, or hurricanes. Similar to the damage inflicted by natural disasters, the damage in Ukraine has been done to a society by an external force: Russia's invasion and way of war in Ukraine have caused massive loss of life, damage to civilian infrastructure—in the areas of housing, transport, commerce, industry, and more—and widespread displacement of people from their homes.[1]

Moreover, the damage done to Ukraine may be repeated in the future if Russia reattacks—a danger that the reconstruction must address. The war in Ukraine may end with a ceasefire or settlement or continue in a low-level fashion, but the threat of renewed Russian attacks will loom. Similarly, most natural disasters last for a limited duration but the threat of the next hurricane or earthquake is often an impetus for building resilience into the new system. In addition, in the case of both disasters and conflicts, communities experience displacement and outmigration. Disasters and conflict alter a population's ability to access critical life-sustaining resources, such as water, housing, jobs, and security.[2] Finally, Ukraine's recovery and

---

[1] World Bank, the Government of Ukraine, and the European Commission, 2022.

[2] See RAND Corporation, *Mass Migration: How RAND Is Addressing One of the Greatest Challenges and Opportunities of the Century*, CP-A715-1, 2020, for a summary of RAND's research on migration resulting from conflict and from climate change and natural hazards.

reconstruction—similar to recoveries and reconstruction from natural hazards—represent an opportunity for the country and its citizens to re-envision the future: Disasters can open new space for investment and allow alternative visions of the country's trajectory to emerge.[3]

The comparison between the two types of events is not perfect, and there are important differences. First, given the scale of Russian attacks in Ukraine, there are few past natural disasters with the same whole-of-economy impact as seen in Ukraine. The impact of Hurricanes Irma and Maria on Puerto Rico is perhaps the best analogy. In September 2022, the Kyiv School of Economics estimated that the total cost of direct documented damage to infrastructure in Ukraine amounted to more than $127 billion.[4] In comparison, the damage to (much smaller) Puerto Rico from Maria was $107 billion.[5] Moreover, given the presence of warring parties, the security needs in post-conflict environments will be more acute than security needs after natural disasters. Options for security arrangements in Ukraine that could deter renewed fighting and allow the work of reconstruction to take place are explored in Chapter 7 of this report. Finally, the physical and mental trauma caused by conflict and invasion will be distinct from that of natural disasters. As one analyst notes, "the challenge of making the population feel safe and secure given the attack from their next-door neighbor is significant. . . . Thousands of Ukrainians of all ages have been killed, leaving many more survivors in mourning."[6]

Although there are clear differences between effects from conflict and disasters, there are useful commonalities between these types of events and the ways in which localities, states, and the international community have managed recovery from them. This chapter reviews some relevant insights and lessons from past disaster recovery experiences that might be useful

---

[3] United Nations, Office for Disaster Risk Reduction, *Build Back Better: In Recovery, Rehabilitation, and Reconstruction (Consultative Version)*, 2017.

[4] KSE Institute, Ministry of Community Development and Territories of Ukraine, Ministry of Infrastructure of Ukraine, and Ministry of Health of Ukraine, 2022.

[5] National Centers for Environmental Information, "Costliest U.S. Tropical Cyclones," fact sheet, National Oceanic and Atmospheric Administration, 2022.

[6] Cynthia Cook, "Rebuilding Ukraine After the War," Center for Strategic and International Studies, March 2, 2022.

to apply to Ukraine's reconstruction, drawing on the general literature and examples from Hurricanes Irma and Maria in 2017 in Puerto Rico and the U.S. Virgin Islands, Hurricane Katrina in 2005 on the United States mainland, the 2010 earthquake in Haiti, the 2011 Christchurch earthquake in New Zealand, and the 2011 earthquake and tsunami in Japan.

In the international context of Ukraine's reconstruction, the U.S. Agency for International Development (USAID) will play an important role, as it did in Central and Eastern Europe and the former Soviet Union in the 1990s and in the Western Balkan Six after the Yugoslavia wars, although not the lead role.[7] In the U.S. context of disaster recovery and reconstruction, the U.S. Federal Emergency Management Agency (FEMA) and the U.S. Department of Housing and Urban Development (HUD) play lead roles, and their practices and procedures provide a strong base of knowledge to apply to international post-war reconstruction. Accordingly, in discussing U.S. cases, this chapter draws on those FEMA and HUD practices.

There are insights and lessons from past disaster recovery and reconstruction experiences, including those in the United States and other national contexts, that might be useful to apply to Ukraine's reconstruction. This section will cover lessons in six thematic areas: setting priorities; funding; donor coordination; local roles and capacity; displaced populations and returns; and transparency, accountability, and data.

Setting Priorities

There are multiple frameworks and toolkits from disasters that may be helpful in prioritizing and funding steps in Ukraine. The disaster community,

---

[7] For examples of the USAID role in reforms in Central and Eastern Europe and the former Soviet Union, see USAID, "Europe and Eurasia," webpage, undated; USAID, "USAID: Partners for Financial Stability (PFS) Program," fact sheet, revised January 20, 2004; Academy for Educational Development, *Final Report: Global Training for Development, January 1997–February 2002*, April 1, 2002; Center for Nations in Transition, Hubert H. Humphrey Institute of Public Affairs, *Final Report of the Environmental Training Project; U.S. Agency for International Development Cooperative Agreement EUR-0041-A-00-2020*, University of Minnesota, Center for Hazardous Materials Research, Institute for Sustainable Communities, and the World Wildlife Fund, September 2001.

including FEMA, the entity in the United States charged with coordinating a federal response to disasters, considers disaster management in five phases: prevention, mitigation, preparedness, response, and recovery.[8] In this case, it is the response and recovery phases that are most relevant. These two phases reflect the fact that in any reconstruction effort, certain tasks must be prioritized, and other tasks must be set aside for later. Response includes those urgent tasks that support people's survival and basic human needs, such as debris removal, sewage repair, electricity, and water.

FEMA's Community Lifelines approach is a framework that can help prioritize tasks within this first crucial response phase. The framework recognizes that unless certain *lifelines* are stabilized within a community (safety; food, water, and shelter; health and medical; energy; communications; transportation; hazardous material), that community cannot begin to recover.[9] These lifelines represent the greatest area of priority and also can serve as indicators of whether a community has stabilized and whether longer-term reconstruction efforts can begin. For example, one of the biggest stumbling blocks to rebuilding Haiti in the aftermath of the 2010 earthquake was removing the tons of rubble left after the earthquake. Whole neighborhoods in Haiti remained choked with debris.[10] Donors did not want to put their money into rubble clearance, but without this, the work of rebuilding government facilities could not begin for months, delaying the entire recovery effort. In Ukraine, immediate priorities will include providing shelters, schools, and basic medical care to help people return, as well as assisting internally displaced people, a topic covered in more detail later in this section. Moreover, mine hazards in Ukraine will pose a significant challenge to reconstruction. The government of Ukraine estimates that 160,000 square kilometers of land may be contaminated by land mines and

---

[8] FEMA, "Mission Areas and Core Capabilities," webpage, last updated July 20, 2020a.

[9] FEMA, "Community Lifelines," webpage, last updated July 27, 2020b.

[10] Tim Padgett, "Haiti's Quake, One Year Later: It's the Rubble, Stupid!" *Time*, January 12, 2011.

other unexploded ordnance.[11] Huge swaths of Ukrainian territory will have to be demined before many recovery tasks can begin.

After the initial response, longer-term recovery can begin with longer-term actions to rebuild the country. Early on, a country's senior political leadership should establish a long-term vision for reconstruction to empower the effort. For example, the strategy for rebuilding after Hurricane Sandy, which struck the New York–New Jersey area as a post-tropical cyclone in October 21012, was widely viewed in the disaster community as a successful recovery. This recovery effort established four overarching principles to "build back smarter and better": recognizing the importance of local inputs, minimizing bureaucracy and maximizing accountability, ensuring a region-wide approach, and rebuilding with resiliency.[12] Similarly, the recovery plan for Puerto Rico in the aftermath of Hurricane Maria oriented the territory's long-term recovery and reconstruction along four primary goals: society, economy, resilience, and infrastructure.[13] Ukraine could benefit from a whole-of-society recovery and reconstruction plan that, in the process of developing the priorities and reimagining the country's trajectory, has a mechanism that includes governmental stakeholders, the private sector, and civil society.[14] Ukraine is doing just that and is likely to continue to modify its plans as the war progresses.[15] Laying out the big choices and decisions that need to be made early on could help to allow Ukraine's leadership to more rapidly galvanize the international community around those choices.

In sum, the disaster community's deep experience with response and recovery has led to useful approaches and frameworks that can help to guide

---

[11] Sergiy Karazy, "Almost One Third of Ukraine Needs to Be Cleared of Ordnance, Ministry Says," Reuters, August 12, 2022.

[12] Hurricane Sandy Rebuilding Task Force, *Hurricane Sandy Rebuilding Strategy: Strong Communities, A Resilient Region*, August 2013, p. 14.

[13] Governor of Puerto Rico and Central Office of Recovery, Reconstruction, and Resiliency, *Transformation and Innovation in the Wake of Recovery: An Economic and Recovery Plan for Puerto Rico*, August 2018.

[14] One analogous mechanism for a whole-of-society effort is the multi-sector accountable body with which and through Millennium Challenge Corporation funding works.

[15] National Recovery Council, *Ukraine's National Recovery Plan*, presentation, Ukraine Recovery Conference, July 2022.

Ukraine's reconstruction. In particular, developing an overarching, whole-of-society plan that considers tradeoffs may help to prioritize and guide recovery.

Funding

The level of available funding might be a constraint for disaster-hit communities. In these cases, external funding is critical. One key challenge in mobilizing external funding is the disparity often seen between pledges and reality—in other words, the difficult task of turning pledges into cash for the reconstruction effort. Direct cash transfers have proven successful in some cases in the immediate humanitarian response to disasters, but donors may be reluctant to fund these devices because of concerns about perceptions of corruption and transparency, as seen in Haiti. Ukraine might face a similar challenge. Another mechanism often used to mobilize external funds after disasters is cost-sharing arrangements. However, experience shows that the recipient often cannot mobilize the required counterpart funding. For example, in Haiti's recovery from the 2010 earthquake, the Oasis Hotel project was meant to fund a major hotel in Port-au-Prince to attract investors, businesses, and donors who needed a safe hotel in which to stay during the recovery efforts.[16] However, the Haitian private-sector investors could not mobilize the total amount of the required share of the equity to enable it to qualify for an International Finance Corporation investment. The Clinton Bush Haiti Fund provided $2 million to partially cover the equity gap, which catalyzed other investments. It is an example of how strategic, but minority, equity funding can help mobilize private sources of funding for important projects and investments. In other words, as Haiti shows, lenders tend to be willing to engage but require equity underneath them.

In other instances, disaster-hit communities may have sufficient funding for recovery but have difficulty spending the money quickly. For example, FEMA obligated $32.3 billion for recovery projects to the governments of Puerto Rico and the U.S. Virgin Islands in response to Hurricanes Irma

---

[16] Business Wire, "Clinton Bush Haiti Fund Invests to Complete Construction of Haitian-Owned Hotel and Conference Center in Port au Prince," May 9, 2011.

and Maria, but only $7.7 billion had been spent as of August 2022.[17] There are likely several reasons for this underspending. First is the lack of capacity in the disaster-hit community to manage the recovery process. Additionally, recovery funding processes and criteria can be onerous, such that navigating them can be very time consuming. In some cases, communities do not have the capacity to absorb the assistance, again slowing down recovery. For example, some communities have significant workforce shortages in comparison with the amount of recovery funding that needs to be spent. In the case of Puerto Rico, shrinking populations and workforce as well as general economic decline made it difficult to spend the unprecedented amount of reconstruction money that was received.[18]

Post-disaster communities also need the proper structures and legal frameworks in which to spend the money. The funding architecture for a recovery and reconstruction effort must be sufficient to the task. Past disaster recovery and reconstruction efforts are replete with funding frameworks that were inadequate and hindered these efforts. For example, during the U.S. government's response to Hurricane Maria in Puerto Rico, policymakers were initially challenged by legal restrictions on FEMA assistance to the territory. Specifically, post-disaster FEMA assistance is not intended to resolve failures of maintenance and neglect. For example, if a community's electric utility generation was undersized for the population that it served prior to the disaster, FEMA cannot provide funds to expand the utility's capacity. But policymakers found that virtually everything in Puerto Rico would have been rendered ineligible for FEMA funding because the territory had not invested in the upkeep of infrastructure before the storm. Rebuilding to the same pre-disaster quality would be a significant disservice to the community. FEMA sought and received additional authority from Congress that was more appropriate to Puerto Rico's circumstances and allowed

---

[17] Chris Currie, *Update on FEMA's Disaster Recovery Efforts in Puerto Rico and the U.S. Virgin Islands*, testimony before the Subcommittee on Economic Development, Public Buildings, and Emergency Management, House of Representatives, September 15, 2022a.

[18] Shelly Culbertson, John Bordeaux, Italo A. Gutierrez, Andrew Lauland, Kristin J. Leuschner, Blas Nuñez-Neto, and Lisa Saum-Manning, *Building Back Locally: Supporting Puerto Rico's Municipalities in Post-Hurricane Reconstruction*, Homeland Security Operational Analysis Center operated by the RAND Corporation, RR-3041-DHS, 2020.

FEMA assistance funds to be used to rebuild to industry standards.[19] Stakeholders involved in Ukraine's reconstruction would benefit from evaluating the frameworks used to authorize assistance and judge whether those are right for the moment and Kyiv's circumstances.

Donor Coordination

Past disaster recovery and reconstruction efforts highlight the importance of having a streamlined command structure to control "donor freelancing" and reduce the burden on the recipient government of interfacing separately with donors.[20]

The influx of funding after a disaster is a tremendously complex burden for recipients to navigate: There are many donors, all with different criteria and monitoring requirements, and all are eager to provide assistance. There is thus a significant risk of overburdening the country's officials. For example, even U.S. federal agencies are not aligned on the same set of conditions and monitoring requirements. A 2022 Government Accountability Office report found that U.S. federal assistance for disaster recovery is extremely fragmented—more than 30 federal agencies that have different priorities, different requirements, and conflicting goals, and all require interaction from affected communities.[21] Fragmentation gets in the way of recovery and

---

[19] Section 20601 of the Bipartisan Budget Act of 2018 (Public Law 115-123, Bipartisan Budget Act of 2018, February 9, 2018) also authorizes FEMA, when using alternative procedures, to provide assistance to fund the replacement or restoration of disaster-damaged infrastructure that provide critical services without regard to pre-disaster condition. The act also authorizes FEMA to fund the repair or replacement of undamaged components of critical services infrastructure when necessary to restore the function of the facility or system to industry standards. See Currie, 2022a.

[20] Organization for Economic Co-operation and Development, *Harmonising Donor Practices for Effective Aid Delivery*, 2003.

[21] Chris Currie, *Disaster Recovery: Actions Needed to Improve the Federal Approach*, Government Accountability Office, GAO-23-104956, November 15, 2022b. RAND research similarly has found that fragmentation among donors was a major obstacle to implementing assistance (Shelly Culbertson, Olga Oliker, Ben Baruch, and Ilana Blum, *Rethinking Coordination of Services to Refugees in Urban Areas: Managing the Crisis in Jordan and Lebanon*, RAND Corporation, RR-1485-DOS, 2016).

prevents communities from receiving assistance. Ukraine's reconstruction similarly will have a wide assortment of donors involved. Without coordination and centralization mechanisms, policymakers can expect that fragmentation will slow the implementation of the reconstruction effort.

In Haiti, the Haiti Reconstruction Fund was established as the major conduit for international assistance, but less than 8 percent of pledged aid during the 2010–2012 period was channeled through this fund. Donors instead channeled funding through nongovernmental organizations (NGOs) and the private sector, which the Haiti Reconstruction Fund could not track or control.[22] A key reason for this was not only donor desire to control and direct funds but also perceptions of corruption and a lack of transparency; both of these are issues that donors will have to grapple with in the context of Ukraine. In the end, the degree to which donor efforts get channeled through a coordinating mechanism will depend on the strength of transparency, anti-corruption, and accountability measures.

Stakeholders involved in Ukraine's reconstruction would also benefit from remaining vigilant about the amount of funding for disaster relief that tends to get stuck in bureaucratic passthroughs of international organizations. For example, one examination of humanitarian aid intended for Syrian refugees in Lebanon and Jordan found that the bulk of assistance, which was allocated to the UN system, was lost on the coordinating system itself (e.g., on staff time, passthroughs by multiple agencies taking a portion, high overhead rates).[23] Ukraine presents an opportunity to streamline and simplify traditional international coordination structures for assistance, potentially by reducing reliance on large bureaucracies, unlocking private-sector sources of funding, and channeling funding in a more direct way to service providers with fewer contracting passthroughs.

---

[22] Jennifer D. P. Moroney, James A. Schear, Joie D. Acosta, Chandra Garber, Sarah Heintz, Jeffrey W. Hornung, Yun Kang, Samantha McBirney, Richard E. Neiman, Jr., Stephanie Pezard, David E. Thaler, and Teddy Ulin, *International Postdisaster Recoveries: Lessons for Puerto Rico on Supply-Chain Management and Recovery Governance*, Homeland Security Operational Analysis Center operated by the RAND Corporation, RR-3042-DHS, 2020, p. 57.

[23] Culbertson et al., 2016.

Simplifying the coordination of assistance delivery might require donors to accept greater risks. For example, the way that FEMA supports the rebuilding of infrastructure after a disaster is facility by facility on a cost-reimbursement basis. At scale, this is a very cumbersome process through which to manage disaster recovery and reconstruction, and the process can obscure opportunities that might exist to reimagine the pre-disaster arrangement of infrastructure in a community. Policymakers may need greater flexibility in applying grant dollars—with appropriate allowances for risks of cost overruns—to encourage local governments to take disasters as opportunities to rethink community institutions during rebuilding.

Local Roles and Capacity

Recovery and reconstruction efforts should be organized to solicit and generate community involvement. Engaging local voices and ensuring that affected communities are intimately involved in the problem-solving and decisionmaking of a recovery and reconstruction effort is a post-disaster best practice.[24] This was a major theme of Puerto Rico's recovery plan. Many earlier successful international recoveries also made this a central tenet. After the earthquake and tsunami in Japan in 2011, multiple participatory mechanisms were used to generate community involvement in reconstruction.[25] Reconstruction also should address local priorities, not just collect local insights. There also needs to be a formal, multi-stakeholder structure created to give local communities and key sectors a sense of ownership and drive buy-in. Local entities should have the lead in implementing reconstruction efforts rather than international NGOs or large contractors. Ukraine might be able to use its impressive digital capabilities to encourage decisions and innovation closer to local populations.[26]

---

[24] Culbertson, Bordeaux et al., 2020.

[25] Naomi Aoki, "Sequencing and Combining Participation in Urban Planning: The Case of Tsunami-Ravaged Onagawa Town, Japan," *Cities*, Vol. 72, Pt. B, February 2018; Moroney et al., 2020, p. 80.

[26] U.S. Agency for International Development, "A U.S.-Supported E-Government App Accelerated the Digital Transformation of Ukraine; Now Ukraine Is Working to Scale

The importance of local involvement can, at times, exist in tension with the reality that local governments may lack the capacity to manage reconstruction processes. This was a significant issue in natural disaster recoveries in the United States: in Puerto Rico, the U.S. Virgin Islands, and New Orleans, to name a few.[27] Many small, rural communities lack the staff, processes, and expertise to manage such large endeavors. Some U.S. communities struggled to participate in FEMA grant programs, unable to even apply for money that could help them because of capacity constraints.[28] Ukraine may face similar capacity challenges. Ukraine is a large country with a highly educated population, but there are reasons to think that its capacity may be stretched: One-third of Ukraine's population has been displaced, presumably including critical personnel, such as local government officials and construction workers; many Ukrainian men have been conscripted into the military and may be wounded; citizens are traumatized and may struggle to organize. Thus, reconstruction in Ukraine will have to balance these competing imperatives of community involvement and capacity of local communities to fulfill their roles, a dilemma that external donors assisting the country's reconstruction should understand.

Displaced Populations and Returns

An important part of Ukraine's recovery from conflict will involve the fate of Ukrainian internally displaced persons (IDPs) and refugees who fled the conflict and are spread elsewhere in Ukraine and throughout Europe. The war has resulted in the largest refugee movements since WWII: There are approximately 5.4 million IDPs across Ukraine and 8 million Ukrainian

---

the Solution to More Countries," press release, January 18, 2023.

[27] Culbertson, Bordeaux et al., 2020, p. 5.

[28] Noreen Clancy, Melissa L. Finucane, Jordan R. Fischbach, David G. Groves, Debra Knopman, Karishma V. Patel, and Lloyd Dixon, *The Building Resilient Infrastructure and Communities Mitigation Grant Program: Incorporating Hazard Risk and Social Equity into Decisionmaking Processes*, Homeland Security Operational Analysis Center operated by the RAND Corporation, RR-A1258-1, 2022.

refugees across Europe.[29] This means that about 35 percent of Ukraine's prewar population (42 million) is now displaced.

Both conflict and disasters lead to people fleeing. Research has shown that there are not many fruitful solutions or a successful track record in getting people to return to their homes in either situation. For example, in an examination of all conflicts since 1980, only about 30 percent of refugees on average return to their countries of origin one decade after a conflict ends.[30] The same study found that the three main reasons for small return numbers included unresolved conflicts; a lack of leadership, funding, and programming to implement the return process; and refugee preference for other solutions (such as the prospect for resettlement in a wealthy democracy). In the case of population loss from disaster, Puerto Rico's population has dropped approximately 12 percent over the 2010–2020 decade, while the rest of the United States grew about 7.4 percent; this is partially because of Hurricane Maria and the subsequent collapse of the territory's economy.[31] In New Orleans, 15 years after Hurricane Katrina, the population still has not returned to pre-hurricane levels.[32]

Ukraine might experience a higher and more rapid rate of refugee return than the modern norm. Ukraine lacks many of the factors that typically have posed greater obstacles to the return of refugees and IDPs, such as insecurity (assuming, as this report does, that a durable post-conflict security arrangement is eventually achieved), societal tensions, and government incapacity. Most Ukrainian refugees and displaced persons seemed to be located only a few hours by train from their homes and are motivated to return.

---

[29] UN, High Commissioner for Refugees, "Operational Data Portal: Ukraine Refugee Situation," webpage, undated; International Organization for Migration, *Ukraine— Internal Displacement Report—General Population Survey Round 12 (16–23 January 2023)*, February 2, 2023.

[30] Constant et al., 2021.

[31] Suzanne Gamboa, "Puerto Rico's Population Fell 11.8% to 3.3 Million, Census Shows," NBC News, April 26, 2021.

[32] Before Hurricane Katrina, New Orleans's population was about 500,000. It dropped to about 250,000 after Katrina, and as of early 2023, is at around 384,000 (Jeff Adelson and Chad Calder, "5 Years On, New Orleans' Uneven Recovery from Katrina Is Complete; Population Slide Resumes," nola.com, January 3, 2022; Allison Plyer, "Facts for Features: Katrina Impact," Data Center, webpage, August 26, 2016.

Moreover, women and children fled Ukraine, while men were not permitted to leave, so there will be pressures for family reunification that might increase returns. But there are other factors that could keep the population from returning. For example, Ukrainians are unlikely to return en masse to areas occupied by Russia. After Russia's incursion into the Donbas and Crimea in 2014, 1.5 million Ukrainians were displaced within the country who have not returned to their homes, and as many as 2 million Ukrainians received visas to work in Poland or were working there informally.[33] Moreover, once refugees put down roots (such as settling children in schools and getting jobs), they face incentives to stay instead of returning home, where they will face destroyed infrastructure, transportation, energy, schools, and hospitals—the rebuilding of which can take a decade or longer.

In short, unless policymakers plan and actively facilitate returns, they will not happen spontaneously at the scale needed to enable recovery. Actively facilitating return will include prioritizing essential tasks even as reconstruction gets going—shelter, schools, and basic medical care—to help people return and assist with IDPs.

Transparency, Accountability, and Data

Accurate data play a critical role throughout the entire life cycle of a recovery and reconstruction effort. At the start of reconstruction, rigorous post-damage assessments are critical to fostering a productive *pull* dynamic from assistance providers. For example, in the aftermath of the Haiti earthquake, assistance flooded the country, but national and local government actors did not feel empowered enough to say no to any expressions of support, even if the support was not fully in step with the country's under-defined, evolving priorities.[34]

During recovery and reconstruction efforts, data-driven metrics and indicators also may be used to measure the progress toward reconstruction and the goals set by the recovery and reconstruction vision. Metrics also

---

[33] Shelly Culbertson and Charles Ries, "Ukraine Invasion Could Spark a Massive Refugee Crisis," *Newsweek*, February 16, 2022.

[34] Moroney et al., 2020, p. 54.

can be used to understand how equitable, timely, efficient, and transparent a recovery and reconstruction effort is.[35] In the aftermath of the 2010–2011 floods and cyclone in Queensland, Australia, the government developed a framework for evaluating recovery outcomes and results called the *Value for Money* approach.[36] In contrast, after the Christchurch, New Zealand, earthquake in 2011, the government measured inputs (e.g., money obligated) rather than outcomes (e.g., the effects achieved) and did not externally report on its performance, making it difficult for stakeholders and the public to assess how effective and efficient the recovery effort was.[37]

Given the scale of reconstruction funds that are likely to flood into Ukraine, Ukraine would benefit from establishing a rigorous framework for monitoring and evaluating the outcome of the funds provided, as discussed further in Chapter 6. This will help to develop the international confidence necessary for reconstruction and help to attract additional capital. Ukraine's need for strong monitoring and evaluation goes well beyond the amount of money that could be at issue. Ukraine's own past issues with corruption and related weak economic and political performance create an argument for rigorous oversight to give investors confidence and maintain international support in the longer term. We now turn to Ukraine's record since independence.

---

[35] Shelly Culbertson, Blas Nuñez-Neto, Joie D. Acosta, Cynthia R. Cook, Andrew Lauland, Kristin J. Leuschner, Shanthi Nataraj, Benjamin Lee Preston, Susan A. Resetar, Adam C. Resnick, Patrick Roberts, and Howard J. Shatz, *Recovery in the U.S. Virgin Islands: Progress, Challenges, and Options for the Future*, Homeland Security Operational Analysis Center operated by the RAND Corporation, RR-A282-1, 2020.

[36] Queensland Reconstruction Authority, *2010/11 Queensland Flood and Cyclone Disaster: Value for Money Strategy*, Queensland Government, undated.

[37] Controller and Auditor-General, *Canterbury Earthquake Recovery Authority: Assessing Its Effectiveness and Efficiency*, New Zealand House of Representatives, 2017.

CHAPTER 4

Planning for Institutional Reform Beyond Infrastructure Repair

Planning for Ukrainian reconstruction should extend beyond repairing the damage done by war to include measures to recover from the 30 years of crony capitalism that preceded it. Just conducting post-war reconstruction will be a challenge. Ukraine, a democratic and European country, will be burdened by memories of its poor economic record and halting efforts to reform its economic policies and strengthen the rule of law.

Ukraine's Economy

Ukraine's economic record since its independence in 1991 has been at or close to the worst of any country of the former Soviet Union or post-communist Central and Southeastern Europe (Figure 4.1). Similar to the rest of the former Soviet Union, it suffered a severe growth collapse in the early 1990s, but it was the only country to experience negative growth in its reported real GDP in every year through 1999, only beginning to experience positive growth in 2000.

As of 2021, Ukraine was the poorest country in Europe (Figure 4.2; this comparison includes Belarus but excludes the countries of the Caucasus and Central Asia). And Ukraine also had the lowest productivity (Figure 4.3).

Furthermore, Ukraine has suffered demographically. It is an aging country: In 1991, Ukraine's population was 51.7 million, of whom 12.6 percent were age 65 or older. In 2014, the year Russia seized Crimea, Ukraine's population was 44.9 million, of whom 15.5 percent were 65 or over. And in 2021, just before Russia's full-scale invasion, Ukraine's population totaled

FIGURE 4.1

Growth of Real Gross Domestic Product Since 1991

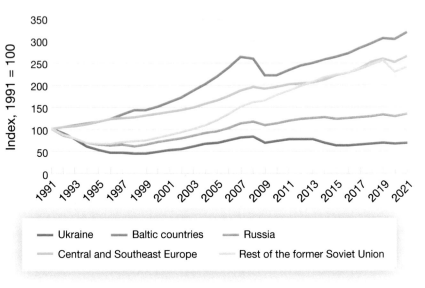

SOURCE: Data from World Bank, December 22, 2022.
NOTES: The variable shown is "GDP (constant 2015 US$)," Series Code NY.GDP.MKTP.KD, Data for the Baltic countries for 1991 through 1994 are not available, so we have imputed those values by using the growth rate of real GDP from 1995 through 2021. In this figure, the Baltics include Estonia, Latvia, and Lithuania. Central and Southeast Europe includes Bulgaria, Czechia, Hungary, Poland, Romania, and the Slovak Republic. Rest of Former Soviet Union includes Armenia, Azerbaijan, Belarus, Georgia, Kazakhstan, Kyrgyz Republic, Moldova, Tajikistan, Turkmenistan, and Uzbekistan.

FIGURE 4.2

Nominal Per Capita Gross Domestic Product, 2021

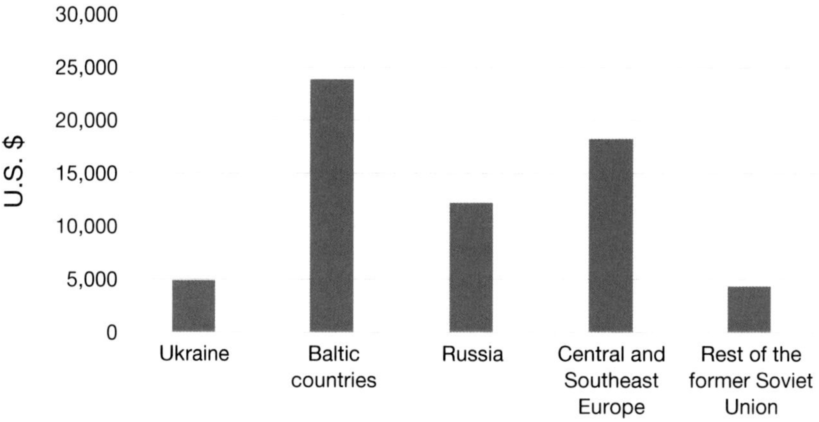

SOURCE: Data from World Bank, December 22, 2022.
NOTE: The variable shown is "GDP per capita (current US$)," series code NY.GDP.PCAP.CD. In this figure, the Baltics include Estonia, Latvia, and Lithuania. Central and Southeast Europe includes Bulgaria, Czechia, Hungary, Poland, Romania, and the Slovak Republic. Rest of Former Soviet Union includes Armenia, Azerbaijan, Belarus, Georgia, Kazakhstan, Kyrgyz Republic, Moldova, Tajikistan, Turkmenistan, and Uzbekistan.

43.7 million, of whom 17.4 percent were 65 or over. Notably, even though the proportion of the population between the ages of 0 and 14 declined following independence, it has recently started rising. In 1991, 21.1 percent were between the ages of 0 and 14. By 2014, this had fallen to 14.9 percent. But in 2021, 16.1 percent of Ukraine's population was between ages 0 and 14.[1]

---

[1] U.S. Census Bureau, "International Database: World Population Estimates and Projections," webpage, last revised December 21, 2021.

FIGURE 4.3

Productivity as Measured by Purchasing Power Parity Gross Domestic Product per Employed Person, 2021

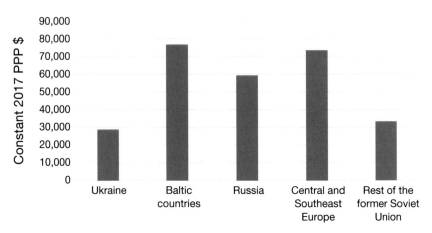

SOURCE: Data from World Bank, December 22, 2022.

NOTE: The variable shown is "GDP per person employed (constant 2017 PPP $)," series code SL.GDP.PCAP.EM.KD. Purchasing power parity (PPP) adjusts GDP to take into account different price levels in a country; for example, a haircut may be cheaper in dollar terms in a developing country than in Europe or the United States, but it is largely an identical service in each country. In this figure, the Baltics include Estonia, Latvia, and Lithuania. Central and Southeast Europe includes Bulgaria, Czechia, Hungary, Poland, Romania, and the Slovak Republic. Rest of Former Soviet Union includes Armenia, Azerbaijan, Belarus, Georgia, Kazakhstan, Kyrgyz Republic, Moldova, Tajikistan, Turkmenistan, and Uzbekistan.

Corruption and Reform Attempts

Two of the biggest inhibitors of economic growth that Ukraine has faced are widespread corruption and control of policy by major businesspeople, known as oligarchs. In 2000, a Harvard University economics professor wrote about Ukraine's pervasive corruption, noting shakedowns by police, extensive tax avoidance, payment of bribes to officials to get investment projects approved, and large-scale theft by senior politicians.[2] In 2014, an economist with long involvement in modernizing post-communist countries noted that endemic corruption was the most important informal insti-

---

[2] N. Gregory Mankiw, "Ukraine: How Not to Run an Economy," *Fortune*, June 12, 2000.

tution in Ukraine and reported that the government at the time believed that senior officials of the previous government had stolen $37 billion from Ukraine over four years.[3] In 2000, Transparency International ranked Ukraine 87 out of 90 countries in its Corruptions Perceptions Index, a widely used measure of corruption present in a country, just above Yugoslavia and Nigeria and tied with Azerbaijan. Ten years later, with many more countries in the index, Ukraine showed modest improvement, ranking a still-low 146 out of 178 (tied with nine countries); its score had risen from 1.5 in 2000 to 2.4 in 2010 (on a scale of one to ten). And in 2020, there again had been some improvement, with Ukraine ranked 117 out of 179 and its score at 33 out of 100. This still put Ukraine lower than almost every former Soviet country (although Russia was ranked lower) and lower than every Central and Southeast European former communist country.[4]

Despite this endemic corruption, there have been efforts to reform the country. Then–Prime Minister Viktor Yushchenko instituted several important reforms related to government operations, the budget, energy, and land in late 1999 and 2000. This spurred Ukraine's first period of economic growth since independence.[5] Other reforms followed, including membership in the World Trade Organization in 2008, tax reform, and a joint stock company law.[6] Reforms accelerated after the so-called Revolution of Dignity in 2014, when Ukraine more firmly linked to the EU and declared its ultimate goal of EU membership.

---

[3] Anders Åslund, "The Maidan and Beyond: Oligarchs, Corruption, and European Integration," *Journal of Democracy,* Vol 25, No. 3, July 2014.

[4] Transparency International, "Transparency International Releases the Year 2000 Corruption Perceptions Index. New Index Is Based on Multiple Surveys from 1998-2000," press release, September 12, 2000; Transparency International, *Corruption Perceptions Index 2010,* September 30, 2010; Transparency International, *Corruption Perceptions Index 2020,* January 28, 2021. The countries ranked below Ukraine in 2020 included Kyrgyzstan, Azerbaijan, Russia, Uzbekistan, Tajikistan, and Turkmenistan.

[5] Anders Åslund, *Why Has Ukraine Returned to Economic Growth?* Working Paper No. 15, Institute for Economic Research and Policy Consulting, July 2002.

[6] Sutela, 2012.

Ukraine has long been an object of competition between Europe and the West on the one hand and Russia on the other.[7] This came to a head in 2013, when Ukraine faced the choice of signing an association agreement and deep and comprehensive free trade agreement with the EU or declining to sign and moving closer to a Russia-centered customs union. When it became apparent that Ukraine would sign the agreements with the EU, Russia started a trade war.[8] The EU association agreement was to be signed in November 2013, but at the last minute, Ukraine reneged, sparking protests that culminated in the collapse of the government and its replacement by a new government, which signed the EU association agreement in March 2014.[9] After a period of provisional application, the agreement entered into force in March 2017.[10]

In the years before Russia's February 2022 invasion, Ukraine continued to make modest progress on reforms but still faced deep economic problems. Privatization of state-owned enterprises—one of the sectors that had large-scale corruption—had not advanced, the private sector had a lack of diversification, and the banking sector was dominated by state-owned banks that had a high proportion of nonperforming loans, which choked finance to private businesses.[11] On the other hand, Ukraine had attained a high average level of education, weaned itself off Russian gas, and instituted a strong legislative agenda, even if implementation was slow.[12]

Shortly before Ukraine signed the EU association agreement in 2014, Russia began an operation that resulted in its annexation of Crimea, followed by its support for separatists in eastern Ukraine and an incursion

[7] Samuel Charap and Timothy J. Colton, *Everyone Loses: The Ukraine Crisis and the Ruinous Contest for Post-Soviet Eurasia*, Routledge, 2017.

[8] Anders Åslund, "Ukraine's Choice: European Association Agreement or Eurasian Union?" Policy Brief No. PB13-22, Peterson Institute for International Economics, September 2013.

[9] Åslund, 2014.

[10] Konstantine Kintsurashvili and Ana Kresic, *Ukraine Diagnostic*, European Bank for Reconstruction and Development, December 2018.

[11] Kintsurashvili and Kresic, 2018.

[12] Kintsurashvili and Kresic, 2018; Pierre Vimont, "Ukraine's Indispensable Economic Reforms," Carnegie Europe, April 29, 2016.

by Russian troops. The post-2014 period illustrates a final challenge for Ukraine's ongoing reform efforts. The low-level war with Russia between 2014 and early 2022 wore on Ukraine's economic progress. Ukraine's military buildup proved costly (although it turned out to have been a wise choice, given Russia's 2022 invasion).[13] The conflict caused emigration and displacement; as many as 2.6 million Ukrainians became IDPs.[14] And while the buildup of Russian troops on Ukraine's border in 2021 prior to Russia's full-scale invasion in 2022 did not cause significant economic problems, it did boost uncertainty and caused the domestic bond market to have temporary outflows.[15] Russia's 2022 invasion caused a contraction of more than one-third in Ukraine's GDP, according to the IMF.[16]

Ukraine's Opportunity to Reform and Rebuild

This review of Ukraine's record since independence suggests three factors that will be important to reform and reconstruction efforts. First, given its past inability to reform and to lower the level of corruption and domination by oligarchs, Ukraine's credibility will be on the line when it comes to administering large-scale funding for reconstruction in the future. Supporting countries will expect concrete reforms. Second, Ukraine's security will prove important both for its own ability to progress and for international business to participate in reconstruction. Finally, Ukraine is facing not only the challenge of post-war reconstruction, but it is also facing the challenge and opportunity of reform to overcome 30 years of underperformance in both economic and political development. In Chapter 5, we turn to how that reform and reconstruction might be financed, and in Chapter 6, to how it might be organized.

---

[13] Vimont, 2016.

[14] Kintsurashvili and Kresic, 2018.

[15] International Monetary Fund, *Ukraine: First Review Under the Stand-By Arrangement, Requests for Extension and Rephasing of Access of the Arrangement, Waiver of Nonobservance of a Performance Criterion, Financing Assurances Review, and Monetary Policy Consultation*, IMF Country Report No. 21/250, November 8, 2021, p. 46.

[16] International Monetary Fund, "How Ukraine Is Managing a War Economy," December 22, 2022b.

CHAPTER 5

Financing

An important issue in planning for Ukraine's recovery, reform, and reconstruction is determining how to mobilize capital for the process. In the end, financing will come from a variety of sources, including official development assistance in the form of grants and loans, private-sector financing in the form of loans and investments, and internal financing mobilized by the Ukrainian government, Ukrainian banks, the Ukrainian business community, and private Ukrainian citizens. Given international precedents, UN General Assembly resolutions, and the moral case for restoring damages caused, compensation funding from Russia should play a role as well and could involve the use of now-frozen Russian international reserves. This chapter reviews several topics in financing reconstruction.

Although this report and this chapter focus on longer-term reform and reconstruction, it should be noted that as of spring 2023, Ukraine had dire immediate needs for assistance.[1] Ukraine has had substantial reserve losses, import compression, and high inflation.[2] Money issuance by the National

---

[1] Maria Repko, "Financing Ukraine's Victory and Recovery: For the War and Beyond," Stockholm Centre for Eastern European Studies, blog post, November 17, 2022.

[2] Robin Brooks[@RobinBrooksIIF], "Ukraine is bleeding official FX reserves (orange) since Russia invaded. Reserve losses are far bigger than they look, as war pushed Ukraine's economy into deep recession, which flipped the current account from deficit into surplus (black). Ukraine urgently needs western cash . . . " Twitter post, November 25, 2022a; Robin Brooks[@RobinBrooksIIF], "When Russia first invaded Ukraine and Russian troops were marching on Kiev, monthly losses in Ukraine's official FX reserves were more than -$4 bn. Putin's rocket attacks on Ukraine to kill its power infrastructure will take us back to that. Ukraine urgently needs western cash. . ." Twitter post, November 25, 2022b; Volodymyr Verbyany, "Ukrainian Inflation Tops 23% As Prices Surge for Seventh Month," *Bloomberg*, September 9, 2022.

Bank of Ukraine to support military and other government spending helps fuel inflation, and lack of ability to repair damaged infrastructure and structures means they are likely to deteriorate, ultimately raising costs of reconstruction.

The Need for Financing

Ukraine has developed a detailed recovery plan with supporting documents that outlines a transformation of the country through 2032.[3] Ukrainians themselves understand the need for both reform and reconstruction. These plans will require major financing, for which Ukraine has proposed sources (Table 5.1). The total sought is greater than $750 billion; Ukraine's proposed plan relies largely on international assistance rather than private-sector participation, although private investment is envisioned as accounting for about one-third of financing, especially in later stages. International bilateral and multilateral assistance is envisioned as more important in the early stages and especially for funding of immediate priorities of ensuring military security, ensuring macro-financial stability (such as through budget support), supporting business and employment, undertaking the repair of major public infrastructure, strengthening the energy sector and logistics resilience, providing support for IDPs and others affected by the war, and minimizing negative environmental consequences.

The international community appears to agree on the need and desirability of international assistance but has avoided large-scale commitments focused specifically on reconstruction thus far, although a great deal of other aid has been delivered. As of late November 2022, the United States had approved $68 billion in three aid packages: The money went toward military assistance, humanitarian assistance, budget support for the government of Ukraine, and U.S. government Ukraine-related operations and domestic costs. This has constituted about 62 percent of all published aid figures.[4] In November 2022, the European Parliament approved an €18 bil-

---

[3]   National Recovery Council, 2022.

[4]   Mark F. Cancian, "Aid to Ukraine Explained in Six Charts," Center for Strategic and International Studies, November 18, 2022.

TABLE 5.1

Illustrative Structure of Funds in the July 2022 Ukraine National Recovery Plan (in billions of U.S. dollars)

Purpose	2022	2023–2025	2026–2032	Total
Partner grants, for example for • defense • emergency budget financing • rebuilding of destroyed housing and infrastructure • enabling and de-risking private investment • infrastructure development with EU structural funds	~60–65	~100–150[a]	~100–150[b]	~250–300
Partner debt and equity, for example for • infrastructure and housing modernization • large-scale energy projects • financial system support • co-financing of private investment		~100–150[c]	~100–150[d]	~200–300
Private investment • co-financing for infrastructure projects • value-adding sectors • other commercially viable investments		>50	>200	>250
Total				>750

SOURCE: Based on and modified from National Recovery Council, 2022, p. 12.
[a] Damaged infrastructure.
[b] Potentially financed via EU Structural Funds, based on Central European countries' benchmarks.
[c] Nondamaged infrastructure assumed, banking system support.
[d] Infrastructure needs, not covered by EU Structural Funds.

lion loan (about $18.5 billion at the time) to cover about half of the monthly funding needed by Ukraine in 2023, although the funding was conditional on implementation of specific reforms.[5] In total, from January 24, 2022, when Russia and Ukraine cut off diplomatic relations, through October 3, 2022, bilateral and multilateral donors had made €92.6 billion ($95.4 bil-

---

[5] European Parliament, "Parliament Approves €18 Billion Loan for Ukraine in 2023," press release, November 24, 2022.

lion) in commitments for financial (49 percent of the total), humanitarian (13 percent), and military (38 percent) assistance.[6]

Countries have started considering longer-term finance for Ukraine's reconstruction. In their final statement, representatives from 41 countries and five international institutions at a July 2022 Ukraine Recovery Conference encouraged all participating countries to financially support Ukraine.[7] As part of this encouragement, they also noted that any financing should be transparent and in accordance with international rules, that there would be accountability for the use of the funding, and that corruption must be eliminated.

International Assistance

It is clear that some form of financing should come as international assistance, either from international or plurilateral institutions, such as the IMF, World Bank, European Investment Bank, or EBRD, or from bilateral assistance and likely from all these sources.

As noted in Chapter 2, in Central and Eastern Europe's transition in the early 1990s, countries faced high levels of debt and adverse balance of payments deficits that limited their abilities to carry out some reforms. Financing from international partners, along with debt relief—including from commercial banks—eased the pressure and allowed countries to make more progress on recovery and restructuring. This was followed by assistance in privatization, especially of state-owned commercial banks, that helped mobilize greater financing from a variety of sources.[8]

International assistance is used for a variety of purposes. When Central and Eastern Europe were undergoing reforms, most early official assistance

---

[6] Arianna Antezza, André Frank, Pascal Frank, Lukas Franz, Ivan Kharitonov, Bharath Kumar, Ekaterina Rebinskaya, and Christoph Trebesch, *The Ukraine Support Tracker: Which Countries Help Ukraine and How?* Kiel Working Paper No. 2218, Kiel Institute for the World Economy, August 2022.

[7] *Lugano Declaration: Outcome Document of the Ukraine Recovery Conference URC2022*, Ukraine Recovery Conference, July 5, 2022.

[8] Roaf et al., 2014, p. x.

went toward budget support, help with balance of payments deficits, and debt relief.[9] Those countries with more-aggressive reforms tended to receive larger flows. But, on average, official flows to Central and Eastern Europe from 1991 to 1993 amounted to about 2.7 percent of the GDP of recipient economies, similar to the relative size of Marshall Plan flows to post-WWII Europe. One difference was that the Marshall Plan, on a relative basis, consisted much more of grants than did the assistance in the early 1990s.[10]

Occasionally, the assistance did not even result in expenditures but rather served as more of a guarantee. For example, when Poland underwent a stabilization program in 1990 to tame hyperinflation and move the zloty quickly to the foreign exchange market, the G7 countries put together a $1 billion stabilization fund to help the country defend its currency at a new exchange rate. This fund did not need to be tapped, and after the program ended, money was repurposed to help recapitalize and then privatize state banks.[11] An equivalent situation applicable to Ukraine reconstruction could be a fund that provides some form of political risk insurance for private-sector investors.

U.S. Enterprise Funds as a Model

International assistance can also be used to fund private-sector development by making equity investments directly in private businesses. One model that might apply to Ukraine reconstruction is an enterprise fund, as developed by the United States in the first wave of Central and Eastern European reforms in 1989. Originally authorized in 1989, the United States eventually set up ten enterprise funds—covering 19 countries and authorizing a total of $1.3 billion in capital—to be used in these countries for loans and equity investments in small and medium enterprises and techni-

---

[9] World Bank, 1996, p. 137.

[10] World Bank, 1996, p. 138.

[11] Louis H. Zanardi, Michael J. Courts, Bruce L. Kutnick, Muriel J. Forster, Bill J. Keller, John D. DeForge, and Walter E. Bayer, Jr., *Poland: Economic Restructuring and Donor Assistance*, General Accounting Office, GAO/NSIAD-95-150, August 1995.

cal assistance.[12] Even more than providing equity capital, the funds could take on the highest-risk positions with a higher risk of loss, especially in small and medium enterprises or smaller reconstruction projects, that most private-sector investors would avoid but that still might prove valuable for the recovering economy. Under independent boards of directors from the United States and host countries, fund senior managers usually were from the United States. The Department of State provided policy oversight while USAID provided operational oversight.

In the end, investments by the funds proved profitable as the economies grew, and after a few years of growth, the U.S. funds generally were able to sell their equity stakes to private investors. Beyond the initial U.S. contributions, the funds reinvested $1.7 billion in net proceeds and raised $6.9 billion in outside capital in the form of debt, equity, and co-investment.[13] Aside from investments, the funds provided $77.7 million in technical assistance. Among the many things that the funds did, they played a role in introducing new financial products, such as home mortgage lending and credit cards. By 2013, the funds had returned $225.5 million to the United States Treasury and were on track to return more than $400 million. The U.S. government, with support from Congress, used the remaining resources (including capital gains) in the funds to endow philanthropic legacy foundations to continue to support reforms and the private sector.

Funding Reconstruction with Russian International Reserves

Another potential source of funding would be compensation from Russia. Small amounts could be allocated in the near term for humanitarian purposes, with larger amounts allocated later for reconstruction. One prominent former policymaker has written that "the G-7 should declare that

---

[12] Jess Ford and A.H. Huntington, III, *Enterprise Funds' Contributions to Private Sector Development Vary*, U.S. General Accounting Office, GAO/NSIAD-99-221, September 1999.

[13] Steve Eastham, David Cowles, and Richard Johnson, *The Enterprise Funds in Europe and Eurasia: Successes and Lessons Learned*, U.S. Agency for International Development, September 12, 2013.

Russia owes compensation to Ukraine under international law."[14] Such compensation could come in the form of reparations, much as the fixed share of oil export revenue that Iraq provided Kuwait following Iraq's August 1990 invasion and its subsequent defeat by a U.S.-led coalition in February 1991.[15] Reparations could involve the use of some portion of Russia's international reserves that were blocked, also referred to as *frozen*, by multinational sanctions in February 2022.[16] On February 18, 2022, just before the start of Russia's invasion, Russia's official international reserves amounted to $643.2 billion.[17] Approximately $300 billion is frozen in Western institutions.[18]

Either of these options—direct transfers funded by oil and gas sales or the use of frozen reserves—could have their own problems.[19] Legal issues regarding the seizure of reserves are complex.[20] This could involve an evo-

---

[14] Robert B. Zoellick, "How the G-7 Can Tip the Scales Toward Ukraine," *Washington Post*, June 26, 2022a.

[15] "Iraq Makes Final Reparation Payment to Kuwait for 1990 Invasion," UN News, February 9, 2022.

[16] Robert B. Zoellick, "Russian Cash Can Keep Ukraine Alive This Winter," *Wall Street Journal*, October 26, 2022b.

[17] Bank of Russia, "International Investment Position on International Reserves of the Russian Federation," spreadsheet, last modified March 9, 2022.

[18] Claire Jones and Joseph Cotterill, "Russia's FX Reserves Slip from Its Grasp," *Financial Times*, February 28, 2022.

[19] The architects of the aggressive, 21st-century U.S. sanctions regime have consistently expressed concern that overuse could ultimately lead countries to seek workarounds that might undermine U.S. leverage in the longer term (Juan C. Zarate, "Sanctions and Financial Pressure: Major National Security Tools," testimony before the U.S. House of Representatives Foreign Affairs Committee, January 10, 2018; Jackie Calmes, "Lew Defends Sanctions, but Cautions on Overuse," *New York Times*, March 29, 2016).

[20] William Courtney, Khrystyna Holynska, and Howard J. Shatz, "Tackling Corruption Is Key to Rebuilding Ukraine," United Press International, April 18, 2022; Philip Zelikow and Simon Johnson, "How Ukraine Can Build Back Better: Use the Kremlin's Seized Assets to Pay for Reconstruction," *Foreign Affairs*, April 19, 2022; Paul Stephan, "Giving Russian Assets to Ukraine – Freezing is not Seizing," *Lawfare* blog, April 26, 2022; Scott R. Anderson and Chimène Keitner, "The Legal Challenges Presented by Seizing Frozen Russian Assets," *Lawfare* blog, May 26, 2022; David Lawder, "Yellen Says Legal Obstacles Remain on Seizure of Russian Assets to Aid Ukraine," Reuters, February 27, 2023.

lution of international law, with a proper finding of aggression by Russia.[21] Finding and using the frozen reserves without agreement by Russia also could have consequences for the operations of the international monetary system, which depends on frequent swap arrangements and balance settlements among central banks, mediated by the IMF and the Bank for International Settlements. Despite discussion of up to $300 billion being available, it is not clear how much of that can actually be located, what entities hold the funds, and what kinds of legal encumbrances those entities are under.[22] Furthermore, it is not even clear what the actual currency composition is because Russia's actual dollar holdings might be higher than it has reported, but it has engaged in foreign exchange swaps to increase its reported holdings of other currencies.[23] Strain on the international monetary system could stimulate, in turn, alternative settlement arrangements and decrease international confidence in the dollar and other Western currencies.[24] An alternative might be to continue blocking the reserves, disallowing their use by Russia or any country, until Russia agrees to a settlement involving

---

[21] Zoellick, 2022b.

[22] Charles Lichfield, "Windfall: How Russia Managed Oil and Gas Income After Invading Ukraine, and How It Will Have to Make Do with Less," Atlantic Council, November 30, 2022; Alberto Nardelli, "EU Urged to Make Banks Report Size of Frozen Russian Assets," *Bloomberg*, February 9, 2023.

[23] Garfield Reynolds, "Pozsar Says $300 Billion Russia Cash Pile Can Roil Money Markets," *Bloomberg*, February 24, 2022; Tracy Alloway and Joe Weisenthal, "Transcript: Zoltan Pozsar on Russia, Gold, and a Turning Point for the U.S. Dollar," *Bloomberg*, March 2, 2022.

[24] The dollar's share in international reserves and international payments has been trending downward for decades, but in both cases the share remains high. For example, in the third quarter of 2022, the dollar constituted almost 60 percent of all global reserves for which a currency was identified, and almost 56 percent of all global reserves (International Monetary Fund, "Currency Composition of Official Foreign Exchange Reserves (COFER)," webpage, last updated December 23, 2022). Likewise, in December 2022, the dollar was used in 42 percent of all global payments, while the Chinese renminbi was used in only slightly more than 2 percent (Society for Worldwide Interbank Financial Transactions [SWIFT], "RMB Tracker," webpage, undated). There are strong arguments about why the dollar will not easily be dethroned, in part because of China's lack of desire or inability to reform its financial system (Michael Pettis, "Will the Chinese Renminbi Replace the US Dollar?" *Review of Keynesian Economics*, Vol. 10, No. 4, Winter 2022).

fair compensation to Ukraine. This amounts to using the frozen reserves as leverage in settlement negotiations.

Notably, in devising a plan for reparations, it will be useful to move beyond the idea that onerous reparations on Germany after World War I were an important reason for that country's turn toward National Socialism in the 1930s.[25] Although the initial reparations amount was defined as a large sum and has been connected to hyperinflation in Germany in the early 1920s, a plan known as the Dawes Plan, led by future U.S. Vice President Charles G. Dawes, was devised in 1923. Using foreign loans, Germany met its reparations obligations in the 1920s, and this enabled other European countries to pay their war debts to the United States. There is a strong case that hyperinflation in Germany had other causes, and the rise of the Nazis was more closely linked to the Great Depression than reparations. The cases of German reparations and Iraqi reparations show that reparations can be assessed and paid—both to help the country that has been attacked and without crippling the country that is being assessed.[26]

Private Investment

Although there is a need for public financing, private investment likely will provide the bulk of reconstruction funding for Ukraine as it did in Japan and Europe after WWII, Central and Eastern Europe, and the Balkans. Ukraine signaled that it is open to foreign private investment and sees it as instrumental in the creation of a new Ukraine. In a September 2022 commentary in the *Wall Street Journal*, Ukrainian President Volodymyr Zelenskyy wrote,

---

[25] However, it is also necessary to say that historians disagree on this point; see, for example, the historians quoted in Isabelle de Pommereau, "Germany Finishes Paying WWI Reparations, Ending Century of 'Guilt,'" *Christian Science Monitor*, October 4, 2010.

[26] For the history of World War I reparations and how they were manageable, see Sally Marks, "The Myth of Reparations," *Central European History*, Vol. 11, No. 3, September 1978; and Office of the Historian, U.S. Foreign Service Institute, "The Dawes Plan, the Young Plan, German Reparations, and Inter-Allied War Debts," webpage, U.S. Department of State, undated.

> I invite foreign investors and companies with ambition to see the advantage in investing in the future of Ukraine, and to recognize the tremendous growth potential our country presents. We have already identified options for more than $400 billion of potential investment, which reach from public-private partnerships to privatization and private ventures.[27]

He noted that USAID has supported Ukraine's Ministry of Economy in setting up a project team of investment bankers and researchers to work with businesses.

In the reform of Central and Eastern Europe in the 1990s, most external capital came as private foreign direct investment (FDI) and commercial bank lending.[28] Much of this FDI was mobilized via privatization, but there was also substantial *greenfield investment*—investment in new ventures. German FDI was particularly important; companies in reforming economies were absorbed into the supply chains of Germany companies. This also boosted exports from the countries that hosted the FDI, particularly in machinery and transport equipment.[29]

Beyond corruption, private investors might face a variety of risks, including political risk. Funds similar to the U.S. enterprise funds formed for post-Soviet reconstruction described previously could help in ameliorating political risk in Ukraine. Publicly supported political risk investment insurance can help attenuate risk. For example, the Multilateral Investment Guarantee Agency, part of the World Bank Group, provides risk insurance to private investors for breach of contract, restrictions on currency convertibility and transfers, expropriation, war and civil disturbance, and the failure of the host governments and state-owned enterprises to honor their financial obligations.[30] A facility dedicated strictly to Ukraine could be established.

Similarly, official funding agencies (such as the EBRD, the European Investment Bank, the World Bank, and the U.S. International Develop-

---

[27] Volodymyr Zelensky, "Invest in the Future of Ukraine," *Wall Street Journal*, September 5, 2022.

[28] Roaf et al., 2014, p. 34.

[29] Roaf et al., 2014, p. 36.

[30] Multilateral Investment Guarantee Agency, "What We Do," webpage, 2023.

ment Finance Corporation) can leverage their assistance and impact by co-financing major infrastructure projects that are Ukrainian priorities, using the format of a managing partner and supporting institutions. That would spread risk and maximize use of agency expertise.

As with official assistance, those countries in Central and Eastern Europe that reformed the most and quickest tended to get a higher proportion of FDI relative to other flows.[31] Reforms that improved the business environment, such as competition policy, proved attractive. Having a functioning manufacturing base also was beneficial. Those without such a base tended to attract FDI in utilities and nontradable sectors (such as services or real estate).

Ukrainian Sources of Finance

Although Ukraine's plans and much international discussion focus on international financing—either in the form of official grants and loans or in the form of private-sector participation—mobilizing Ukrainian capital will be important. Domestically sourced investment either from the private sector or the government was important to financing recovery and reconstruction after WWII and after the liberation of Central and Eastern Europe and the end of the Soviet Union.

Willingness to mobilize domestic finance could have the added benefit of building confidence among foreign financial sources. Furthermore, it would give Ukrainians more control and flexibility of the recovery, reconstruction, and redevelopment of their country.[32]

Despite the importance of locally sourced financing, it is unlikely that much of the investment capital could be funded by the regular government budget. In 2019, the last full year before the coronavirus disease 2019 (COVID-19) pandemic, Ukraine government revenues totaled $37 billion and expenditures totaled $40 billion.[33] Furthermore, mechanisms that con-

---

[31] Roaf et al., 2014, p. 34.

[32] Courtney, Holynska, and Shatz, 2022.

[33] Toma Istomina, "Ukraine Ends 2019 with Smaller Budget Deficit Than Expected," *Kyiv Post*, January 3, 2020.

sist of monetary base expansion—essentially printing money—could result in high or hyperinflation, as occurred in Japan after WWII and Central and Eastern Europe at the end of the 1980s. Accordingly, the government contribution likely will need to come from bond issuance; the bonds would be sold either to the Ukrainian public or international buyers.

Because of limits on the government's ability to finance reconstruction, the Ukrainian private sector will need to mobilize financing. It is likely that international donors will expect the Ukrainian private sector to do so as well. In this case, co-financing through equity investments or loans, such as by foreign enterprise funds or bilateral or multilateral institutions, could help support local investments.

In addition, although not strictly local, the large Ukrainian diaspora can play a role in funding reconstruction and business activity. One estimate from before Russia's 2022 invasion noted that the diaspora ranged from 7 million up to 20 million, and there were more than 1,000 Ukrainian diaspora organizations worldwide. Furthermore, these organizations already had been active in humanitarian response in Ukraine before 2022, suggesting that they have already established networks that can be used for reconstruction and investment.[34]

---

[34] Diaspora Emergency Action and Coordination Platform, *Diaspora Organizations and Their Humanitarian Response in Ukraine,* U.S. Agency for International Development and Danish Refugee Council, June 2021.

CHAPTER 6

Organizing the Effort

Successful reform and reconstruction of Ukraine will require the mobilization of unprecedented quantities of external and internal financial resources; a broadly shared vision for Ukraine's future (in the region and in the global community); and effective coordination of the interests and support domestically within Ukraine and with the EU and European countries more broadly, the United States, and other international partners with major stakes in the outcome (such as Japan, Australia, Turkey, and the Gulf countries). It will also require a secure environment, which we discuss in Chapter 7.

As examined earlier, in previous, ambitious joint international efforts at aiding post-conflict, post-disaster, and post-transition reconstruction, the international community experimented with various strategies to mobilize and channel help to affected regions, prevent waste and corruption, and steer reconstruction efforts to achieve optimal outcomes. Help for a post-conflict Ukraine, while unique in some ways, should be designed in light of what the international community has learned from past experiences.

As the war rages, Ukraine and the international community are afforded the time—although perhaps not the policy focus—to consider and put in place principles and mechanisms to coordinate reconstruction efforts for the next phase of Ukraine's history. In this chapter, we lay out coordination principles and discuss how implementation might be organized, internationally and within the U.S. government, in light of prior reconstruction efforts.

First Principles for Coordination

Agreement on why and how to assist Ukraine should be a starting point for the international community, preceding deep engagement on specifics, quantities, and modalities for assistance, or on sectoral priorities. The following concepts can be organizing points for such first principles.

Ukraine sets the priorities. Fighting a challenging and brutal war while preserving its democratic system and institutions should earn Ukraine the right to set its priorities—and those of the international community—for rebuilding. In the security sphere, Ukraine will need to design durable defense structures against future Russian aggression, including air defense, cyber, and basing arrangements, and assess which Western weapons systems it will need. Ukraine's partners can advise and help forecast possible defense technology developments and will retain sovereign defense technology controls and decisions. But the Ukrainian defense forces' innovative and flexible conduct of the war should give Ukraine the lead role in conceptualizing and designing the way the country will build a credible layered defense against its northern neighbor in the future. As with Israel, Ukraine's international partners should give real deference to Ukraine's assessments of which Western weapons systems it will need. We provide additional detail on what such security arrangements might look like in Chapter 7.

In the economic and social policy realms, deference to Ukrainian priorities would include space to make and take responsibility for such sensitive economic choices as (1) how much to invest in Ukraine's heavy industry, (2) the economic basis for its infrastructure rebuilding (e.g., such questions as whether to use autoroute or bridge tolling, the designs for electricity and gas utility structures), or (3) methods for the restructuring of state-owned enterprises. As a prospective member of the EU, Ukraine will need to meet its accession criteria and abide by its constraints on state enterprises (among many other laws and rules). But despite temptations otherwise, European and U.S. advisers should let the Ukrainians debate and decide sensitive structural socio-economic policies.

The EU should be the lead international economic partner; the United States should be the lead security partner. Even if it is indisputable that Ukrainians set the priorities, among international partners, a practical division of labor would facilitate effective support for reconstruction. Because the EU is a major trading partner for Ukraine and Ukraine is aspiring to EU membership, it would make sense for the EU to take the lead in engaging and supporting the Ukrainian government, private sector, and civil society in the socio-economic sphere.

By the same token, the United States and the United Kingdom have been the leading suppliers of vital military equipment to the Ukrainian defense forces during the present conflict, as coordinated by U.S. European Command (EUCOM), the U.S. regional headquarters in Stuttgart. The United States accordingly should continue to lead in planning the support of Ukraine's defense in the post-war period. While it might be tempting to have NATO play this role, that would needlessly raise Russian paranoia levels, and, in any case, there will likely be participation by non-NATO members as well. Leadership of the effort to safeguard Ukraine's security does not necessarily prejudge the specific arrangement that the United States, its allies, and Ukraine formulate. We discuss these options in Chapter 7.

In each domain—the EU in economics, the United States in security—this principle is about leadership, not participation. There should be effective involvement by the EU, other partners, and the United States in all aspects of the implementation and real contributions to benefit Ukraine's objectives in these fields. Even in the economic domain, however, timing also matters. In previous major multilateral efforts, such as support for Central and Eastern European democracy in the 1990s, the United States was able to make a major contribution by appropriating and obligating critical assistance quickly, which was followed up in the same sectors with larger, longer-term commitments from the EU and other partners.

In addition, the international financial institutions (such as the World Bank, IMF, EBRD, and the European Investment Bank) will need to provide billions in major project financing and their indisputable policy analysis experience. The international financial institutions and other assistance-providing countries, such as Japan, the United Kingdom, Canada, and Australia, also should have seats at the economic assistance coordination table. It is even conceivable that China would want to take part, and if so, it should be welcomed (as long as its credit terms are concessionary and take on the same seniority as all other bilateral assistance) because China's participation would further isolate Russia.[1]

Reconstruction is more than funding new capital investment: Current operations matter too. The disruptions to Ukraine's economy and impaired fiscal position will continue even once the active shooting stops. In the war's phase as of late 2022, the government of Ukraine had been receiving Western transfers for current operations on the order of $5 billion monthly. When the reconstruction period begins, the economy and tax revenues will recover, but not immediately. There will still be an urgent requirement for fiscal transfers to support government operations essential to ensure a smooth transition to the reconstruction phase (and there inevitably will not be a bright line between the relief and reconstruction phases). It is also important to support clearing operations in the interest of rebuilding and public safety and to foster the political sense that things are changing.

Ukrainian and International Mechanisms

Although it is important for Ukraine and its international supporters to agree on principles for post-war reconstruction, the design (and use) of effective coordination mechanisms also is essential to ensure that these principles result in action. Previous international assistance efforts have modeled various means of bringing about such coordination and unfortunately, at times, modeled dysfunction and ways to dissipate international enthusiasm.

International experience (such as Poland's post-1989 record) would suggest that the Ukrainian government should place one senior minister in overall charge, with the mandate to establish priorities, direct national resources, engage with Ukraine's parliament, and interface with Ukraine's international partners, including making commitments consistent with

---

[1] Even with the EU in the lead for reconstruction coordination, one option to ensure coordination of financing is to work through a World Bank trust fund. The World Bank runs a variety of trust funds and has the benefit of robust expertise regarding reconstruction and the ability to coordinate regional development banks and multiple donors. This would also avoid fragmentation that could result from bilaterally funded projects and help ensure accountability and payment safeguards. See World Bank, "Trust Funds and Programs," webpage, 2023.

conditionality. A ministerial committee would not substitute for a single ministerial coordinator, but it could help in ensuring that the minister in charge can convey priorities to the wider government. At the same time, it will be important to strike a balance between centralized and decentralized decisionmaking in Ukraine. Decentralization reforms in Ukraine gave more responsibility for services to local authorities.[2] Local governments are widely seen as the engines for competition and experimentation. Furthermore, cities might not fully trust Kyiv and the central ministries that they perceive to be corrupt. The challenge for Ukraine will be to design a coordination mechanism that encourages—rather than stifles—local innovation.

For the partners, periodic donor conferences are not enough to effectively work with Ukraine: Empowered representatives of supporting institutions, including the international financial institutions, should be appointed and in daily contact with Ukrainian authorities. In addition to senior officials in capitals, donors and international financial institutions should appoint senior representatives to reside in Kyiv (for socio-economic reforms) or at EUCOM's Stuttgart headquarters (for defense and security reforms and rebuilding). Agreement among donors and lenders on conditionality, especially in relation to Ukraine's EU aspirations, is critical. In this, non-EU members should follow the EU's lead.

Ensuring the reconstruction process is not excessively burdened with corruption, waste, fraud, or abuse will be vital to maintain support domestically and internationally. Valid perceptions of corruption and a weak rule of law might seriously impede both aid flows and FDI. Ukraine should appoint a senior and independent inspector general with the authorities necessary to ensure that contracting is transparent and responsible, and this office should be supported by embedded international experts appointed and supported by Ukraine's donors. Furthermore, Ukraine's efforts should be public, robust, and transparent to overcome international skepticism. Given past corruption in the country, there are legitimate doubts about the extent to which this problem can be reduced, especially if the international com-

---

[2] Balázs Jarábik and Yulia Yesmukhanova, "Ukraine's Slow Struggle for Decentralization," Carnegie Endowment for International Peace, March 8, 2017; International Republican Institute, "Research from Four Cities in Ukraine Highlights Importance of Decentralization," November 8, 2019.

munity is willing to overlook some amount of malfeasance for geostrategic goals. However, an independent institutional mechanism backed by strong international oversight has not previously existed. In addition, reconstruction will take years and comes with a high risk of donor fatigue, and a major corruption scandal could easily fracture donor support.[3]

In addition, mobilizing international support, maximizing domestic political engagement, and deconflicting initiatives will require full transparency about the effort. Objective, consistent, and current data indicators should be assembled, managed, and published separately from the reconstruction policy process.

For this purpose, and separate and apart from an inspector general function focused on waste, fraud, and abuse, reconstruction in Ukraine should include an internationally supported effort at monitoring and evaluation of project and program support activities. A monitoring and evaluation effort would be focused on whether the policy approaches are *effective* in achieving the outcomes sought. Many assistance agencies and development banks routinely conduct independent monitoring and evaluation studies, but by coordinating and sharing these analyses among Ukraine's ministries, assistance partners, and engaged NGOs, the monitoring and evaluation effort can foster transparency and learning from approaches that work (and those that do not).

Among the international partners for Ukraine, there should be a special council to foster cooperation with its key neighbors, especially Poland, Bulgaria, Moldova, Romania, and Turkey. As explained in Chapter 2, the Marshall Plan support for rebuilding of post-war Europe was conditioned on participation in regional cooperation entities, such as the European Iron and Steel Community. There is considerable scope for similar mutually beneficial initiatives (e.g., in transport, agriculture, energy, heavy industry) between Ukraine and its immediate neighbors.

To provide the Ukrainian government with economic policy expertise and support, the OECD should consider establishing a special standing committee of member-state policy officials to serve as a think tank and sounding board for Ukrainian ministries.

---

[3] Joshua Rudolph and Norman L. Eisen, "Ukraine's Anti-Corruption Fight Can Overcome US Skeptics," *Just Security*, November 10, 2022.

And finally, a coordination and discussion body should be established to open lines of communication and policy insights among the Ukrainian government ministries, supporting international donors and international financial institutions, and Ukrainian and international civil society, business and NGOs directly involved in reconstruction.

Organizing the U.S. Government to Help

The U.S. government has capacity, funding, and expertise spread across dozens of departments and specialized agencies that will be helpful to Ukraine's reconstruction. Yet, as Washington policymaking veterans can attest, the U.S. government is so large that disagreements or priority mismatches among cabinet departments or between the executive and legislative branches can work against even the highest priority missions.

In 1989, the administration and the Congress worked together to enact the Support for East European Democracy (SEED) Act.[4] This landmark bill, initially focused on Poland and Hungary—but in subsequent years expanded to cover the rest of the Central and Eastern European countries— was designed to support democratic institutions and free-market activities. An important bureaucratic innovation of the SEED Act was the designation of a SEED program coordinator with oversight over all aspects of the effort.[5]

The SEED coordinator, initially Deputy Secretary of State Lawrence Eagleburger, mobilized the bureaucratic and financial resources of the administration to help the Central and Eastern European countries. The SEED coordinator had authority to reallocate funding from USAID to other agencies based on needs; interface with Congressional appropriators and authorizers; and, through special notwithstanding authority, could autho-

---

[4] Enacted as Public Law 101-179, Support for Eastern European Democracy (SEED) Act of 1989, November 28, 1989.

[5] "Policy coordination of SEED Program: The President shall designate, within the Department of State, a SEED Program coordinator who shall be directly responsible for overseeing and coordinating all programs described in this Act and all other activities that the United States Government conducts in furtherance of the purposes of this Act" (Pub. L. 101-179).

rize activities consistent with the act's purposes, notwithstanding other provisions of law.

Three years later, in 1992, Congress passed the Freedom for Russia and
Emerging Eurasian Democracies and Open Markets (FREEDOM) Support
Act.[6] This followed the dissolution of the Soviet Union at the end of 1991 and
was aimed at Russia and 11 other former Soviet entities, including Ukraine
(the three Baltic countries, never recognized as part of the Soviet Union by
the United States, were covered in separate legislation).[7] The act authorized
the use of SEED Act funds for countries covered by the FREEDOM Support
Act.[8] Furthermore, similar to the SEED Act, the FREEDOM Support Act
designated a coordinator, also initially Eagleburger (who delegated many of
these powers to deputy coordinator Richard L. Armitage) with the so-called
notwithstanding authority.[9]

The Ukraine reconstruction assistance effort would benefit greatly from
the authorization of a similar senior coordinator role within the U.S. government, which could then effectively interface with international assistance and security activities and ensure the consistency of this reconstruction effort with U.S. foreign policy priorities. Vesting all funding and policy
oversight in one office and working within the National Security Council–led interagency process would ensure that the U.S. view was well rep-
resented and effectively deployed in the field, in Brussels EU councils, and
in Washington.[10] And the coordinator could keep congressional committees full apprised and consulted on all aspects of the reconstruction process,
which will be vital for maintaining funding and policy consistency.

The selection of an official who is well and favorably known across
Washington would also be important to achieving these goals. This was
true of Paul Hoffman's leadership of the Marshall Plan's Economic Coordi-

---

[6] Public Law 102-511, FREEDOM Support Act, October 24, 1992.

[7] Curt Tarnoff, *The Former Soviet Union and U.S. Foreign Assistance in 1992: The Role
of Congress,* Congressional Research Service, RL32410, May 20, 2004.

[8] Congressional Research Service, "Summary: S.2532—102nd Congress (1991–1992):
Conference Report Filed in House," October 1, 1992.

[9] Tarnoff, 2004, pp. 5, 17–18.

[10] The coordinator, for example, could prepare and co-chair National Security Council
Deputies Committee meetings on Ukraine reconstruction topics.

nation Administration and Eagleburger's coordinator role for the SEED and FREEDOM Support Acts. Ideally, such a coordinator would be a Senate-confirmed ambassador, who, while supported by the State Department, would also have direct White House access.

These same principles of leadership apply to the EU as much as they do to the United States. As with the United States, the EU likely would benefit from establishing a unique, time-limited coordinating entity that is not part of one of the European Commission's existing directorates-general, led by an official with similar freedoms to those accorded to the U.S. coordinator. The European Commission has done this in the past, most recently by appointing Michel Barnier as chief negotiator for the exit of the United Kingdom from the EU, with the rank of director-general and a direct reporting line to the president of the European Commission.[11]

Finally, the importance of public and congressional support for Ukraine's reconstruction cannot be understated. As noted in Chapter 2, the Truman administration's extensive efforts to secure buy-in from Congress and the American people and assure them that the Marshall Plan—which would cost taxpayers $13 billion—was workable and would benefit them was among the reasons for the plan's success. Ukraine's reconstruction will take a long time. U.S. public support for Ukraine cannot be taken for granted. Already, there are signs from some corners that public and congressional support for Ukraine is eroding.[12] A growing share of Republicans say the United States is providing too much support to Ukraine.[13] Maintaining sustained support and attention over years—or even more than a decade—will similarly necessitate a skillful, well-orchestrated campaign that spans presidential administrations.

---

[11] European Commission, "President Juncker appoints Michel Barnier as Chief Negotiator in Charge of the Preparation and Conduct of the Negotiations with the United Kingdom Under Article 50 of the TEU," press release, July 27, 2016.

[12] Kurt Schlichter, "Ukraine's Friends May Doom It—and Us," *Townhall*, February 23, 2023; Neil Patel, "How to End the Ukraine War," *Daily Caller*, February 23, 2023.

[13] Amina Dunn, "As Russian Invasion Nears One-Year Mark, Partisans Grow Further Apart on U.S. Support for Ukraine," Pew Research Center, January 31, 2023.

CHAPTER 7

Securing a Rebuilt Ukraine

Most analysis of Ukraine's reconstruction revolves around economics and governance, often neglecting the security dimensions of reconstruction. But as our historical cases have shown, security is a basic prerequisite for the successful execution of reconstruction in Ukraine. In Japan, a new U.S.-Japan security treaty provided the necessary stability for economic takeoff. NATO provided security for transformative European reconstruction efforts after WWII, after the Cold War, and after the wars in the Western Balkans.

Without durable post-war security arrangements, economic recovery and political development in Ukraine could come under great strain. Reconstruction progress could be subject to military attack. Investors would be reluctant to accept the risks involved while the Ukrainian government gives priority to preparing for renewed conflict. Provisions for security are therefore an essential component of any reconstruction plan. In this chapter, we examine several alternative approaches to post-war security arrangements designed to facilitate longer-term reconstruction and secure a more peaceful and prosperous future for Ukraine.

Ukraine as an Integral Part of the European Security Architecture

Ukraine—a capable military power on Russia's border—has become and will remain an important factor in the European power balance. On the one hand, Russia's invasion of Ukraine seems likely to produce a security situation in Europe that is highly unfavorable to Moscow. Russia's military setbacks in the war, the Kremlin's isolation from the economically advanced countries, and tough economic sanctions degrade Russia's strategic position relative to the United States and Europe.[1] Unless it is utterly defeated, Ukraine's westward drift will remain firmly secured. If NATO allies deliver on their pledges to increase defense spending and capabilities, the conventional military balance in Europe will continue to shift to Russia's disadvantage.[2] Russia's own military faces constraints that will be difficult to overcome, stemming from troop and equipment losses sustained during the war and its cut-off from advanced technology from the West.[3] Meanwhile, NATO had added Finland and will add Sweden, two highly capable militaries that can enhance the alliance's defense and deterrence capabilities, especially in the Baltic Sea region.[4]

On the other hand, no matter how well Ukraine does on the battlefield, the United States and Europe still might face a potentially unstable situation. A post-conflict environment in Ukraine may involve an ever-present risk of renewed Russian military aggression. While locking in most of the security advantages that will have accrued to it, the West should aim to reduce longer term volatility and forestall prospects of another devastating conflict. Thus, the West's strategy, in close coordination with Kyiv, should be to forge postwar security arrangements that deter Russia, strengthen Ukraine's defenses, and motivate both sides to keep the peace.

Security Arrangements for a Rebuilt Ukraine

At the time of this writing, Ukraine had achieved impressive battlefield success while Russia had significantly underperformed in the war. It is possible that Russia might be decisively defeated or decide to withdraw from Ukraine, its forces overwhelmed with little capacity to continue. It is also

---

[1] Samuel Charap and Michael J. Mazarr, "The Wisdom of U.S. Restraint on Russia," *Foreign Affairs*, September 12, 2022.

[2] Eugene Rumer and Richard Sokolsky, "Putin's War Against Ukraine and the Balance of Power in Europe," Carnegie Endowment for International Peace, April 11, 2022.

[3] Dara Massicot, "Russia's Repeat Failures: Moscow's New Strategy in Ukraine Is Just as Bad as the Old One," *Foreign Affairs*, August 15, 2022.

[4] Gene Germanovich, "Finnish and Swedish NATO Membership: Toward a Larger, Stronger, Smarter Alliance," United Press International, August 12, 2022.

possible that Russia may decide to escalate the war rather than capitulate. Nevertheless, unless Ukraine can mount a successful invasion of Crimea, which will be very difficult, the war might end in a ceasefire or armistice that defers the permanent resolution of the territorial status of Crimea.[5] The outcome of the war is thus unlikely to fully satisfy either side, no matter which emerges on top.

Case studies of previous conflicts have shown that belligerents who have recently fought each other will remain intensely antagonistic and inclined to renew the conflict at some stage.[6] The absence of fighting may be taken by one or both parties as an opportunity to reconstitute forces for a future offensive to pursue a more favored outcome. A cessation of hostilities between Russia and Ukraine may leave both sides intensely dissatisfied. Peace will endure only if it appears to both Moscow and Kyiv as preferable to renewed conflict.

Ukraine will have powerful positive incentives to keep the peace as it mounts a massive internationally assisted reconstruction effort and moves toward membership in the EU. Russia, under its existing leadership, will have no such opportunities. Moscow's adherence to any peace agreement will depend heavily on the additional level of deterrence and defense capability provided by the United States and its allies to support the maintenance of peace.

What Level of Deterrence Is Enough?

Deterrence aims to alter the perceived costs and benefits of going to war. The costs of renewed conflict—political, military, and economic—must

---

[5] A grand political settlement between Russia and Ukraine on the issues over which the war has been fought is very unlikely. See Clint Reach, "Obstacles to Lasting Peace Between Ukraine and Russia," *Santa Monica Daily Press*, July 7, 2022.

[6] This was the case with Minsk II, a hastily drafted and bitterly disputed agreement, negotiated in 2015 to stop fighting in the Donbas (Duncan Allan, *The Minsk Conundrum: Western Policy and Russia's War in Eastern Ukraine*, Chatham House, May 2020; see also Virginia Page Fortna, "Scraps of Paper? Agreements and the Durability of Peace," *International Organization*, Vol. 57, No. 2, 2003, p. 350).

outweigh expectations of any benefits to be gained by resuming fighting.[7] Thomas Schelling describes two forms of deterrence: by denial and by punishment.[8] In post-conflict Ukraine, deterrence by denying Russian objectives seems most promising, given Ukraine's performance on the battlefield and its sustained Western support. Deterrence by punishment may be less viable because of Ukraine's limited capacity to strike Russian territory, NATO concerns about conflict escalation, and the Russian capacity to withstand punishment. Therefore, the focus here is on deterrence by denying Russia's ability to achieve its military objectives in Ukraine.

So how much deterrence will be sufficient to prevent renewed war in Ukraine? Among the courses of action open to them, the United States and its allies could:

1. commit to providing continued material support to Ukraine's defense
2. threaten to introduce Western forces into Ukraine in the event of renewed Russian aggression
3. bring Ukraine into NATO.

These three courses of action are not mutually exclusive, and all three could be pursued. The first represents continuity with existing policy. The West can provide peacetime Ukraine with the aid it needs to quickly rebuild its forces and establish a robust defense against another potential attack from Russia. Recent analysis notes that to build a modern military capable of defending Ukraine in the long term, Kyiv needs a high-readiness force that can effectively and forcefully respond to a territorial breach, a training and joint maneuver program, advanced anti-access and area-denial sys-

---

[7] As James Fearon explains, war is *ex post inefficient*. Unless fighting is preferred for its own sake, even enemies would prefer to settle their disputes without resorting to war (James D. Fearon, "Rationalist Explanations for War," *International Organization*, Vol. 49, No. 3, 1995).

[8] Thomas Schelling, *Arms and Influence*, Yale University Press, 2008.

tems, access to the EU's capability funding, and a large self-defense territorial force.[9]

The strength of this approach is that a modernized, capable Ukrainian military is the most straightforward and arguably most effective means to deter Russia. Direct deterrence by denying Russia an ability to achieve military objectives in Ukraine (Ukraine places significant military capabilities directly in the path of Russia) is more reliable than extended deterrence by punishment (Ukraine's allies or partners threaten to respond in some way if Russia re-attacks Ukraine).[10] Russia might doubt the West's ability or willingness to collectively impose its threatened punishment. Ukrainian military capabilities speak for themselves, especially given Ukraine's relative success since the February 2022 invasion.

In addition to sustaining and perhaps expanding the existing military supply relationship, the United States and its allies could warn that renewed Russian aggression might lead to the entry of Western forces into Ukraine. This could be signaled both in declaratory policy and visible preparations for such a move. This approach may lack credibility, however, because Western leaders individually and NATO collectively have been clear that they will not take this step in response to Russia's 2022 invasion. Such promises from individual NATO member-states could jeopardize the cohesion of the alliance in supporting Ukraine and present openings for Russian interference to divide NATO politically.

Finally, Ukraine might be brought into NATO. This step offers the surest guarantee of effectual support in the event of another Russian attack. Moreover, by joining NATO, Ukraine—thanks to the modern, Western assistance that it has successfully absorbed and skillfully employed—would provide the alliance with one of the most capable armies in Europe.[11] NATO successfully provided security for transformative European reconstruction

---

[9] Office of the President of Ukraine, "Andriy Yermak and Anders Fogh Rasmussen Jointly Present Recommendations on Security Guarantees of Ukraine," September 13, 2022.

[10] Michael J. Mazarr, *Understanding Deterrence*, RAND Corporation, PE-295-RC, 2018, p. 2.

[11] Steven Erlanger, "What Does It Mean to Provide 'Security Guarantees' to Ukraine?" *New York Times*, January 10, 2023.

efforts after WWII, after the Cold War, and after the Western Balkan wars. It might be the best answer again this time. However, Ukraine's accession to NATO does face some obstacles that policymakers would benefit from considering. For example, NATO membership requires the consent of all 31 present NATO members, which might be difficult to achieve. NATO's commitment at the 2008 Bucharest Summit—that Ukraine (and Georgia) will become members of the alliance—has been reaffirmed repeatedly, but no practical measures have been taken to fulfill the commitment because there is no consensus among the alliance to do so.[12] Even in the face of overt Russian aggression in Ukraine, any political initiative to bring Ukraine into NATO could lead to internal divisions, eroding the solidarity of NATO and continued support to Ukraine, and not result in consensus. The net effect could be to reduce deterrence of further Russian aggression. Events have demonstrated that NATO has grown powerful enough to deter Russia even while helping Ukraine turn back the Russian attack. And Ukraine has proved capable of doing so with only material assistance from NATO countries. Therefore, expanding NATO might not be necessary to preserve the favorable European balance.

Is Deterrence Enough?

Deterrence can be strengthened by moving beyond the supply of materiel, advice, and financial support to the possible commitment of Western forces to Ukraine or a full NATO Article V guarantee for Ukraine. However, if deterrence fails, these steps make it less likely that the fighting would be confined to Ukraine. Moreover, even with deterrence, it might be possible to have too much of a good thing. The classic security dilemma posits that perfect security for one side can mean total insecurity for the other, causing the weaker party to undertake desperate measures to avoid that fate.[13] Thus, Russia may balk at concluding a peace agreement if such an agreement were accompanied by NATO membership for Ukraine. An aggressive, irredentist

---

[12] NATO, "Bucharest Summit Declaration," April 3, 2008.

[13] Robert Jervis, "Cooperation Under the Security Dilemma," *World Politics*, Vol. 30, No. 2, January 1978.

regime like Putin's might be tempted to break out of any peace that subsequently led to this outcome.

This suggests that one must look beyond deterrence for additional measures to bolster the fragile peace likely to emerge from this conflict. For any post-war security arrangement to endure, it must contain provisions that both parties value over continued fighting.[14] Ukraine will have very attractive alternatives to renewed fighting as it launches an ambitious reconstruction effort and pursues its quest for EU membership. Given Moscow's unprovoked invasion of a peaceful country and its conduct of the war, neither Ukraine nor its Western backers will be inclined to offer Russia comparable incentives to keep the peace.

One alternative that policymakers might consider is some form of multilateral security guarantee. Multilateral security guarantees typically involve a promise of mutual restraint toward a state: The recipient of the guarantee commits to some behavior, while the guarantors pledge to respect the sovereignty of the recipient if their rival does the same. One plausible permutation of a multilateral security guarantee could be one in which Ukraine commits to being a neutral country. In this case, the promise by the guarantors would not just be to respect Ukraine's neutrality but to help defend it, even against another guarantor. Individual countries could decide if they wanted to opt into the arrangement as guarantors. Ukraine's guarantors could either be a grouping of Western countries or include a broader set of countries that includes Russia. In either permutation, the intention would be clear: Ukraine would be defended if Russia violated its territorial integrity. In the event of an attack on Ukraine, the guarantor states would be committed to aid in its defense, perhaps in the same manner as the United States and its allies are in the present conflict. The advantage of this policy option is that Ukraine could be confident of Western assistance if attacked, while Russia could be confident of Ukrainian neutrality if Ukraine is not attacked, thus giving Russia a positive stake in keeping the peace.

These guarantees could be codified in a legally binding UN Security Council resolution (unlike the failed Budapest Memorandum, which was

---

[14] Suzanne Werner, "The Precarious Nature of Peace: Resolving the Issues, Enforcing the Settlement, and Renegotiating the Terms," *American Journal of Political Science*, Vol. 43, No. 3, July 1999.

only a political document).[15] Such an arrangement for Ukraine might be reinforced by renewing broader regional confidence-building agreements, starting with the Vienna Document.[16] With the status of Ukraine agreed and secured, NATO-Russia relations could be renewed by way of the NATO-Russia Council, reciprocal liaison missions, and transparency measures for military postures on both sides.

Ukraine, of course, will have the leading role in conceptualizing and designing the most appropriate arrangements for its post-war security; the United States and the European countries will support Ukrainian priorities. It is not clear that such a multilateral security guarantee would have support among Ukraine's leadership or public. Earlier in the war (March 2022), when Ukraine's military prospects were less favorable, Russia and Ukraine held peace talks in Istanbul, during which Ukrainian diplomats introduced a framework under which Ukraine would remain neutral, with its security guaranteed by various Western partners and by Russia.[17] President Volodymyr Zelenskyy personally endorsed this proposal that month.[18] The Ukraine-Russia talks in Istanbul ended without a result. Ukraine is again seeking NATO membership, and its leaders have been silent on the concept

---

[15] In the 1994 Budapest Memorandum, the United States, the United Kingdom, and Russia promised to respect Ukraine's sovereignty and territorial integrity. In return, Ukraine pledged to give up its nuclear weapons and join the Nuclear Non-Proliferation Treaty. According to senior Ukrainian diplomats who were involved in the negotiations, there was also an implicit—though never documented—assumption in the memorandum that Ukraine would be nonaligned (Jeremy Shapiro, James Dobbins, Yauheni Preiherman, Pernille Rieker, and Andrei Zagorski, "Regional Security Architecture," in Samuel Charap, Jeremy Shapiro, John Drennan, Oleksandr Chalyi, Reinhard Krumm, Yulia Nikitina, and Gwendolyn Sasse, eds., *A Consensus Proposal for a Revised Regional Order in Post-Soviet Europe and Eurasia*, RAND Corporation, CF-410-CC, 2019, pp. 20–21).

[16] The Vienna Document dates to 1990, with successor documents in 1992, 1994, and 1999, with subsequent amendments. It is a confidence-building agreement related to the transparency of conventional forces among members of the Organization for Security and Cooperation in Europe (Arms Control Association, "The Vienna Document," fact sheet, updated February 2023).

[17] Farida Rustamova, "Ukraine's 10-Point Plan," *Faridaily* blog, March 29, 2022.

[18] Camille Gijs, "Zelenskyy: Ukraine Ready to Discuss Neutral Status to Reach Russia Peace Deal," *Politico*, March 28, 2022.

of neutrality. Neutrality also does not enjoy support among the majority of the public.[19]

Kyiv does support a proposal, the Kyiv Security Compact, jointly developed by former NATO Secretary-General Anders Fogh Rasmussen and Head of the Office of the President of Ukraine Andriy Yermak. The proposal calls for Ukraine to receive Western security guarantees, not as an alternative to NATO but as a way station while Ukraine continues to pursue membership.[20] The compact rules out neutrality, noting that the guarantees should not "be drawn in exchange for a specific status, such as neutrality, or put other obligations or restraints on Ukraine."[21]

Is There a Special Place for Ukraine in the European Order?

Since the breakup of the Soviet Union, Ukraine's position has been recognized as unique because of its size, location, and history. However, the existing architecture for European security offers only a binary choice: join an alliance or you are on your own. Ukraine has never quite fit into this model. Now, in the wake of Russia's invasion, Ukraine and the Western powers aiding it have begun to carve out a third way, one in which a state victim of aggression can receive assistance without forming a permanent attachment. Can existing arrangements for supporting Ukrainian defense be developed into credible guarantees for its post-war security? Could this provide a long-term place for Ukraine in the European order? NATO membership might well be the most suitable choice to guarantee Ukraine's security and the security of Europe. But this conclusion is best tested by evaluating alternatives.

---

[19] According to an October 2022 survey conducted by the Kyiv International Institute of Sociology and funded by the Norwegian Refugee Council, over 60 percent of Ukrainians do not favor neutrality (Kristin M. Bakke, Gerard Toal, John O'Loughlin, and Kit Rickard, "Putin's Plan to Stop Ukraine Turning to the West Has Failed—Our Survey Shows Support for NATO Is at an All-Time High," *The Conversation*, January 4, 2022. See also Tom Balmforth, "Ukraine Applies for NATO Membership, Rules out Putin Talks," Reuters, September 30, 2022).

[20] Office of the President of Ukraine, 2022.

[21] Office of the President of Ukraine, 2022.

Sanctions as Deterrents and Incentives

Military posture and security architecture are two elements of a U.S. strategy to alter Russia's perceived costs and benefits of returning to war. Sanctions are another. Sanctions can and usually do have multiple aims, including compliance, subversion, deterrence, and symbolism.[22] The United States and its allies placed a series of sanctions on Russia following its 2014 annexation of Crimea, its war in eastern Ukraine, and its interference in the 2016 U.S. presidential elections. U.S. and European officials hoped that these measures would not only punish Russia for such actions but also deter Russia from escalating its assault on U.S. and European interests.[23]

In the lead-up to Russia's 2022 invasion of Ukraine, the United States and its allies sought to deter Moscow by threatening to impose more sanctions if Russia invaded. The threat of sanctions is often more effective than their actual imposition because the actual imposition of sanctions represents a failure in strategy on both sides (with the target of sanctions underestimating the resolve of the sender to impose the sanctions, and the sender being unable to persuade the target that it would be better off changing course than paying the price of the sanctions).[24] But the threat of sanctions failed to deter Russia from invading Ukraine. In any event, the sanctions that the West imposed after Russia's invasion were much more severe than the sanctions that were publicly threatened before the invasion (for example, on February 24, President Joe Biden publicly ruled out removing Russia from SWIFT, the global messaging system that banks use to transfer money; however, two days later, the United States, along with its European partners, had SWIFT remove selected Russian banks).[25]

---

[22] For more on the uses of sanctions, see Howard J. Shatz and Nathan Chandler, *Global Economic Trends and the Future of Warfare: The Changing Environment and Its Implications for the U.S. Air Force*, RAND Corporation, RR-2849/4-AF, 2020, p. 85.

[23] Peter Harrell, "How to Hit Russia Where It Hurts," *Foreign Affairs*, January 3, 2019.

[24] Thomas Biersteker and Peter A. G. van Bergeijk, "How and When Do Sanctions Work?" in Iana Dreyer and José Luengo-Cabrera, eds., *On Target? EU Sanctions as Security Policy Tools*, European Union Institute for Security Studies, 2015, p. 22.

[25] Gerard DiPippo, "Deterrence First: Applying Lessons from Sanctions on Russia to China," Center for Strategic and International Studies, May 3, 2022; White House,

Once imposed, sanctions can lead to changes in behavior on the part of the target only if the target believes that if it complies with the demands, the sanctions can and will be lifted. However, the West likely will face a dilemma in which Russia presumably will still be deserving of sanctions and taking actions that require some of the sanctions to be left in place. Yet, there could be a strong case for partially lifting sanctions in response to specific Russian actions so that Moscow sees that there is value to complying and not reattacking Ukraine. Sanctions could be lifted incrementally depending on the original rationale for imposing them. For example, sanctions imposed on Russia because of its annexation of Crimea in 2014 likely would remain in place as long as Russia holds the territory. Some post–February 24, 2022, sanctions could be lifted when a cessation of hostilities is reached to incentivize Russia to not renew the war. Still other sanctions could be lifted if Russia compensates Ukraine for damages caused during the war.

It follows that the West could then devise a way to agree a priori to snap back any lifted sanctions if Russia renews war in Ukraine. In addition to the snap back of current sanctions, more–severe economic measures—such as a complete trade embargo and a complete cutoff of the Russian financial sector—could be applied to increase the cost of any new Russian aggression. The United States, the EU, other G7 members, and other sanctioning countries might want to devise various hand-tying mechanisms that would commit them to reimposing sanctions under certain conditions. This could signal to Moscow the strength of the shared commitment. In the United States, for example, an independent commission created by Congress with members appointed by Congress and the President could publicly report on Russian compliance every six months to highlight compliance and the threat of snap back, thereby creating pressure. A statement from the G7 countries and NATO also could lay the groundwork for a snap back of sanctions.

"Remarks by President Biden on Russia's Unprovoked and Unjustified Attack on Ukraine," February 24, 2022; European Commission, France, Germany, Italy, United Kingdom, Canada, and the United States, "Joint Statement on Further Restrictive Economic Measures," February 26, 2022.

CHAPTER 8

A Freer, More Prosperous, and Secure Future for Ukraine and Its Partners

Military momentum had turned in favor of Ukraine by late 2022: By November, Ukraine's armed forces had taken back more than half the land that Russia had conquered earlier in the war.[1] On the other hand, the war might still be in its early stages, unpredictable events can happen, and the Russian armed forces may yet find advantages on the battlefield.[2]

The United States has a strong interest in the outcome of the war, specifically in an outcome that is favorable to Ukraine. Such an outcome would increase European security and even global security by showing that aggression, in this case on the part of Russia, does not provide benefits to the aggressor. Depending on the details of the outcome, an outcome favorable to Ukraine could increase the count of strong, Western-oriented, market-based democracies that subscribe to the Western-led rules-based international order. And there would even be a chance, however small, that an extension of a prosperous Europe—whole and free, stretching to the shores of the Don River—could prove an attractive force for Russia to become less repressive and less aggressive and pursue a greater stake in the global system for the benefit of the Russian people.

---

[1] Scott Reinhard, "Ukraine Has Reclaimed More Than Half the Territory Russia Has Taken This Year," *New York Times*, November 14, 2022.

[2] David E. Johnson, "This Is What the Russians Do," *Lawfire* blog, Duke University, May 3, 2022.

But the prospects for such a result will depend on many factors, from Kremlin liberalization to the successful reform and reconstruction of Ukraine. And that, in turn, will involve a complex web of multiple countries and international institutions with an array of choices to make.[3] In this final chapter, we review the key findings that we have derived from relevant past examples of reconstruction following wars, system changes, and natural disasters.

Lessons from Past Post-War Reform and Reconstruction Efforts

Capital shortages appear to have been a key constraint always and everywhere. But post-war and post-disaster reconstruction events show that there are better and worse ways to mobilize capital, just as there are better and worse ways to organize reconstruction.

The post-WWII reconstruction of Europe and Japan and post-war reconstruction of the Balkans demonstrated the importance of security guarantees and even troop presence. In fact, there is evidence, at least in post-WWII Europe, that the absence of security guarantees in 1946–1947 led to stalled reconstruction. Durable security arrangements can give the private sector greater confidence to risk investment.

Given security, conditionality in the disbursement of financial assistance played an important role. This was notable in the Marshall Plan for post-WWII Europe and in the success of Central and Eastern Europe after 1989. In the former case, conditionality was sometimes applied selectively to ensure the success of the most important policy goals. In the latter case, EU conditionality and the desire of those countries to join provided a strong impetus to internal reforms. However, conditionality without a timetable, as in the case of the Western Balkans, weakens the power of conditionality to

---

[3] One way to think about the many choices to make during the reconstruction process is to arrange them in four categories: (1) When and how fast? (2) Who directs? (3) Who, where, and what to focus on? (4) Who pays? For more on this, see Khrystyna Holynska, Jay Balagna, and Krystyna Marcinek, *The Trade-Offs of Ukraine's Recovery: Fighting for the Future*, RAND Corporation, RR-A2370-1, 2023.

move reforms forward. In the case of Ukraine, donors might coordinate to adopt the same conditions on their assistance: Those conditions would be the EU membership criteria that Ukraine must meet.

The ability to trade internationally proved important in all cases. Marshall Plan conditionality encouraged greater intra-European trade. Japan's recovery was aided by production for the Korean War, and then at the end of the 1950s, by the opening of U.S. markets and finance. For the Central and Eastern European countries after 1989, the Europe Agreements were particularly important in providing industrial free trade with the EU, which proved critical for driving investment and incentivizing structural reform, such as the shutdown of inefficient heavy industry. Along with trade, cross-country infrastructure connections, such as gas, roads, and electricity, promoted regional cooperation.

In the specific case of Ukraine, following Russia's annexation of Crimea in 2014, the EU first liberalized trade through an association agreement, ratified in 2017, and through an additional three years of unilateral additional market access measures. Through the 2022 invasion by Russia, the EU had liberalized market access to Ukraine's trade but also tightened access in certain cases; however, on balance, the EU liberalized much more than it tightened.[4] The path to EU membership will include further liberalization, with membership resulting in full admission to the EU customs union and free trade. The United States will not be able to negotiate a separate free trade agreement with Ukraine once it is an EU member—the EU has a common trade policy for all members—but should Ukraine not join, a U.S.-Ukraine free trade agreement might be considered. The importance of trade and investment, the proximity of Ukraine to the EU, and the EU's external leadership of reform and reconstruction with the potential for EU membership also highlight that EU members will need to match actions with commitments and that failure to do so will hurt the EU's strategic interests and its goals of strategic autonomy.

Just as access to international markets was necessary, so too were internal reforms, often resulting from conditionality. In almost all cases, internal stabilization was required—specifically, bringing down high inflation and

---

[4] Simon Evenett, "Trade Policy and Deterring War: The Case of Ukraine Since the Annexation of Crimea," Global Trade Alert, February 14, 2022.

rectifying problems with public finances, as in the case of Japan with the Dodge Line. But in all cases, more fundamental reforms were needed. Such reforms were exemplified by the Central European countries of Poland, Czech Republic, and Hungary, which undertook deep reforms following their exits from the Soviet orbit, thereby unleashing domestic private investment and attracting foreign direct investment.

Lessons from Post–Natural Disaster Reconstruction Efforts

The task of rebuilding Ukraine also can be compared to recovery from natural disasters, such as fires, earthquakes, tsunamis, and hurricanes. Similar to the conflict in Ukraine, disasters can leave in their wake enormous levels of infrastructure damage, damage to social and economic systems, and the widespread displacement of people from their homes. But destruction from natural disasters provides an opportunity for a country to re-envision its future: New infrastructure can be built, better and more–energy-efficient housing and offices can be built, and a variety of other improvements can be made that might be more difficult without the domestic urgency and international assistance that come with reconstruction.

Throughout disaster recovery episodes, sequencing of reforms proved important. In Haiti, for example, delays in tackling simple tasks, such as rubble removal, stalled recovery. In Ukraine, the immediate problem will be the removal of mines and unexploded ordnance. Funding structures for reconstruction also must be sufficient to the task: In some cases, the challenge will be mobilizing sufficient external funding and turning pledges into cash. In other cases, funding might be widely available, but disaster-hit communities will not be able to absorb the assistance, which can slow recovery. Past disaster recovery efforts also highlight the importance having a streamlined command structure to control donor freelancing and reduce the burden on the recipient government of interfacing separately with donors.

The most successful disaster recovery efforts address local priorities and ensure affected communities are intimately involved in the problem-solving and decisionmaking processes. But the importance of local involvement exists in tension with the reality that local governments might lack the capacity to manage reconstruction processes. Reconstruction in Ukraine will have to balance the competing imperatives of community involvement and the capacity of local communities to fulfill their reconstruction roles.

Ukraine also will have to contend with large numbers of IDPs and refugees who fled the conflict and are spread elsewhere in Ukraine and throughout Europe. Returns will not happen spontaneously at the scale needed to enable recovery unless policymakers plan and actively facilitate them. Doing so requires sequencing and prioritizing essential tasks as reconstruction gets underway—e.g., shelter, schools, basic medical care—to help people return.

Financing

Ukraine's financing needs will be quite large, perhaps multiples of its prewar GDP over the course of the decade following a settlement of the war. The open question is from where that financing will come. It will need to come from a variety of sources: bilateral and multilateral grants and loans, international private-sector investment and loans, Ukrainian domestic investment and savings, and Ukrainian national and local government finance. The amounts from each are uncertain, although it is worth remembering that Marshall Plan aid amounted to only 2.6 percent of the GDP of the 16 recipient countries, and official flows to Central and Eastern Europe from 1991 to 1993 amounted to about 2.7 percent of the GDP of recipient economies.

In 2021 dollars, Marshall Plan spending was about $128 billion, far less that some estimates for spending on Ukrainian reconstruction. There is a risk that Ukrainians might expect the monetary value of assistance to be a multiple of Marshall Plan aid and be disappointed if it does not materialize. Donor countries will also have their own domestic spending priorities, which could become more acute if the West were to slip into recession.

Regardless of the amounts of aid provided, a variety of steps can help unleash private-sector investment. For Ukraine, these include improved rule-of-law and anti-corruption measures and strong dispute settlement procedures, such as through the World Bank Group's International Centre for the Settlement of Investment Disputes. From the realm of international assistance, these steps might involve (1) enhanced investment and risk insurance and (2) co-investment, as exemplified by the U.S. enterprise funds in the 1990s or the case of the Oasis Hotel project in Haiti after the 2010 earthquake there.

One other important medium-term decision will be whether to seize frozen Russian international reserves and private-sector assets prior to a post-war settlement. There are strong moral and practical arguments for using the roughly $300 billion in frozen reserves and a portion of some $1 trillion in private-sector assets to help Ukraine repair damages caused by Russian forces and start rebuilding.[5] Seizure and use of the assets would be considered fair by Western parliaments that otherwise strain to fund arms and assistance for Ukraine.

But seizure and use of the frozen assets—especially the official international reserves—would have downsides as well. In the United States, there is not a clear legal basis for seizure of official assets of a country with which the United States is not at war. Accordingly, new legislation authorizing the transfer of seized reserves to an international fund for Ukraine might be needed. Doing so could expose Western assets to retaliatory expropriation in the future and could be a further incentive for countries that have unstable relations with the United States to bypass the U.S.-led international financial system.[6] In any case, while seizing these assets would provide Ukraine with near-term funding, it would have no effect on Putin's war effort because Russia cannot use them. The frozen assets also might be used as leverage in post-war settlement and reparations arrangements.

Congressional pressure for forfeiture of Russian assets may be strong. The Consolidated Appropriations Act for federal fiscal year 2023 included an amendment that allows the attorney general to transfer to the secretary of state forfeited property controlled by a person subject to sanctions to provide assistance to Ukraine.[7] Accordingly, this will need to be settled as reconstruction planning proceeds.

---

[5] Zoellick, 2022b. See also Timothy Ash, "Allocate Frozen Russian Assets to Ukraine Now!" *@tashecon* blog, January 16, 2023.

[6] "Why the West Should Be Wary of Permanently Seizing Russian Assets," *The Economist*, June 19, 2022. See also Elizabeth Braw, "Freeze—Don't Seize—Russian Assets," *Foreign Policy*, January 13, 2023.

[7] Public Law 117-328, Consolidated Appropriations Act, 2023, Division M, Additional Ukraine Supplemental Appropriations Act, 2023, Title VII, Department of State and

Organizing the Reconstruction Effort

Reconstruction planning and implementation will require considerable coordination. Past post-war and post-disaster reconstruction events provide useful guidance.

There inevitably will be a multitude of interested parties, so clear leads and lines of reporting will be important. Ukraine should set the priorities. The Ukrainians have paid the most, in lives lost and disrupted, infrastructure destroyed, and economic damage. Beyond that, they will have the best understanding of their country's needs, what might be politically possible, and how best to implement policies within the Ukrainian system.

Internationally, the United States will need to take the lead on security, much as it did in Europe and Japan after WWII and in the Balkans in the 1990s. Likewise, the EU will need to take the lead on economic assistance and political reform, not least because Ukraine is now a candidate country for EU membership and will require EU assistance and support to succeed.

But this does not mean the major powers should work separately. It will be helpful for the United States to participate in economic restructuring (following the EU's lead) and for the European countries to participate in security provision (following the lead of the United States).

Furthermore, there will need to be an on-the-ground presence with considerable authority. For the United States, appointing a procurement coordinator with notwithstanding authority as with the SEED and FREE-DOM Support Acts, as described in Chapter 6, can remove bureaucratic roadblocks that stand in the way of implementing even a widely agreed-on policy. Furthermore, ongoing engagement with the U.S. Congress will be important for a U.S. coordinator, and ongoing engagement with the European Parliament is likely to be important for the EU lead.

Data, monitoring, and evaluation will prove essential to ensuring that reconstruction is proceeding as well as possible. However, the data, monitoring, and evaluation function should be kept separate from the policy development and implementation function. An independent inspector-general system also will be necessary, both for preventing and exposing

---

Related Agency, Section 1708, December 29, 2022.

waste, fraud, and abuse and producing useful reports that build confidence in the reconstruction effort.

Ukraine's economy might not improve immediately following the end of the active conflict. The government of Ukraine has been receiving Western transfers for current operations of around $5 billion monthly. When reconstruction begins, the economy and the country's tax revenues will recover, but not immediately. Thus, there will still be a pressing requirement for fiscal transfers to support government operations that are essential to ensuring a smooth transition to the reconstruction phase.

Security

Previous post-conflict reconstruction efforts—and even post–natural disaster efforts where domestic insecurity was present—show that security is an integral component of any reconstruction effort. Prior European reconstruction efforts were secured by NATO membership and NATO peacekeepers. Japan's strongest economic takeoff period came on the heels of a new security treaty with the United States.

Providing security to Ukraine in a post-war environment will be challenging because the outcome of the war is unlikely to fully satisfy either side. Both Russia and Ukraine might retain incentives to renew the fighting at some stage. Ukraine, for its part, will have an attractive alternative to renewed conflict in consolidating its Western orientation and moving toward EU membership. Russia, at least under its current leadership, will have no such prospects, and its adherence to any peace agreement will depend heavily on the level of deterrence provided by the United States and its allies.

In terms of deterrence, among the courses of action open to them, the United States and its allies could commit to providing continued material support to Ukraine's defense, threaten to introduce Western forces into Ukraine in the event of a renewed Russian aggression, or bring Ukraine into NATO. Higher levels of deterrence might make renewed fighting less likely, but if deterrence fails, the higher levels of deterrence that had been provided might also make the resultant conflict less likely to be limited to Ukraine. Moreover, these options can strengthen deterrence but also might decrease Russia's perception of its own security, perhaps leading it to take destabilizing measures in response. This suggests that U.S. policymakers should look beyond deterrence to additional measures to bolster the fragile peace likely to emerge from this conflict. Such measures might include a multilateral security arrangement in which Ukraine's security is guaranteed by a grouping of nations.

The existing architecture for European security—either in NATO or not in NATO—offers a binary choice. Ukraine and the Western powers aiding it have begun to carve out a third way. Whether that is sufficient to provide credible guarantees for Ukraine's post-war security cannot yet be determined and may depend on war termination.

Preparing for Reform and Reconstruction

Significant reform and major reconstruction might not be able to start in earnest until the war draws to an end or a stalemate, but there is much that can be done in the near term. Steps that should be taken soon include determining the organization of the international effort, including passing any necessary legislation; agreeing to methods of finance, including passing authorizing legislation for allocating financial assistance or establishing purpose-built institutions; and working with Ukraine to establish an agreed sequencing, especially under the assumption of constrained financing.

For Ukraine, important steps that should be taken, even during wartime, are reconsidering the enabling environment for financing and investment, strengthening anti-corruption efforts, and enhancing the rule of law. Even if Ukraine emerges victorious, potential bilateral donors already have multiple calls on their resources, not least investing in their own economies in the wake of difficult economic times related to COVID-19 pandemic–related supply and demand disruptions and aggravated by the repercussions of Russia's invasion of Ukraine.

Helping Ukraine reform and reconstruct will be in the interest of the United States and the West. Ukrainian reforms can increase the chances that the United States and the West will follow through on those interests and help Ukraine fulfill its own post-war vision.

Abbreviations

COVID-19	coronavirus disease 2019
EBRD	European Bank for Reconstruction and Development
EU	European Union
EUCOM	U.S. European Command
FDI	foreign direct investment
FEMA	Federal Emergency Management Agency
FREEDOM	Freedom for Russia and Emerging Eurasian Democracies and Open Markets
G7	Group of Seven
GDP	gross domestic product
IDP	internally displaced person
IMF	International Monetary Fund
NATO	North Atlantic Treaty Organization
NGO	nongovernmental organization
OECD	Organisation for Economic Co-operation and Development
OEEC	Organisation for European Economic Co-operation
SCAP	Supreme Commander of Allied Powers
SEED	Support for Eastern European Democracy
SWIFT	Society for Worldwide Interbank Financial Transactions
UN	United Nations
USAID	U.S. Agency for International Development
WWII	World War II

References

Academy for Educational Development, *Final Report: Global Training for Development, January 1997–February 2002*, April 1, 2002.

Adelson, Jeff, and Chad Calder, "5 Years On, New Orleans' Uneven Recovery from Katrina Is Complete; Population Slide Resumes," nola.com, January 3, 2022.

Allan, Duncan, *The Minsk Conundrum: Western Policy and Russia's War in Eastern Ukraine*, Chatham House, May 2020.

Alloway, Tracy, and Joe Weisenthal, "Transcript: Zoltan Pozsar on Russia, Gold, and a Turning Point for the U.S. Dollar," *Bloomberg*, March 2, 2022.

Anderson, Scott R., and Chimène Keitner, "The Legal Challenges Presented by Seizing Frozen Russian Assets," *Lawfare* blog, May 26, 2022.

Antezza, Arianna, André Frank, Pascal Frank, Lukas Franz, Ivan Kharitonov, Bharath Kumar, Ekaterina Rebinskaya, and Christoph Trebesch, *The Ukraine Support Tracker: Which Countries Help Ukraine and How?* Kiel Working Paper No. 2218, Kiel Institute for the World Economy, August 2022.

Arms Control Association, "The Vienna Document," fact sheet, updated February 2023.

Aoki, Naomi, "Sequencing and Combining Participation in Urban Planning: The Case of Tsunami-Ravaged Onagawa Town, Japan," *Cities*, Vol. 72, Pt. B, February 2018.

Ash, Timothy, "Allocate Frozen Russian Assets to Ukraine Now!" *@tashecon* blog, January 16, 2023. As of February 14, 2023: https://timothyash.substack.com/p/allocate-frozen-russian-assets-to

Åslund, Anders, *Why Has Ukraine Returned to Economic Growth?* Working Paper No. 15, Institute for Economic Research and Policy Consulting, July 2002.

Åslund, Anders, "Ukraine's Choice: European Association Agreement or Eurasian Union?" Policy Brief No. PB13-22, Peterson Institute for International Economics, September 2013.

Åslund, Anders, "The Maidan and Beyond: Oligarchs, Corruption, and European Integration," *Journal of Democracy,* Vol. 25, No. 3, July 2014.

Bakke, Kristin M., Gerard Toal, John O'Loughlin, and Kit Rickard, "Putin's Plan to Stop Ukraine Turning to the West Has Failed—Our Survey Shows Support for NATO Is at an All-Time High," *The Conversation*, January 4, 2023.

Balmforth, Tom, "Ukraine Applies for NATO Membership, Rules out Putin Talks," Reuters, September 30, 2022.

Bank of Russia, "International Investment Position on International Reserves of the Russian Federation," spreadsheet, last modified March 9, 2022.

Barnes, Julian E., "Putin Wants to Take Most of Ukraine, but a Quick Breakthrough Is Unlikely, the Top U.S. Intelligence Official Says," *New York Times*, June 29, 2022.

Barro, Robert J., "Rare Disasters and Asset Markets in the Twentieth Century," *Quarterly Journal of Economics*, Vol. 121, No. 3, August 2006.

Becker, Torbjörn, Barry Eichengreen, Yuriy Gorodnichenko, Sergei Guriev, Simon Johnson, Tymofiy Mylovanov, Kenneth Rogoff, and Beatrice Weder di Mauro, eds., *A Blueprint for the Reconstruction of Ukraine*, Centre for Economic Policy Research Press, April 5, 2022.

Beckley, Michael, Yusaku Horiuchi, and Jennifer M. Miller, "America's Role in the Making of Japan's Economic Miracle," *Journal of East Asian Studies*, Vol. 18, No. 1, 2018.

Biersteker, Thomas, and Peter A. G. van Bergeijk, "How and When Do Sanctions Work?" in Iana Dreyer and José Luengo-Cabrera, eds., *On Target? EU Sanctions as Security Policy Tools*, European Union Institute for Security Studies, 2015.

Braw, Elizabeth, "Freeze—Don't Seize—Russian Assets," *Foreign Policy*, January 13, 2023.

Brooks, Robin [@RobinBrooksIIF], "Ukraine is bleeding official FX reserves (orange) since Russia invaded. Reserve losses are far bigger than they look, as war pushed Ukraine's economy into deep recession, which flipped the current account from deficit into surplus (black). Ukraine urgently needs western cash . . . " Twitter post, November 25, 2022a. As of November 28, 2022: https://twitter.com/RobinBrooksIIF/status/1596181898988081155

Brooks, Robin [@RobinBrooksIIF], "When Russia first invaded Ukraine and Russian troops were marching on Kiev, monthly losses in Ukraine's official FX reserves were more than -$4 bn. Putin's rocket attacks on Ukraine to kill its power infrastructure will take us back to that. Ukraine urgently needs western cash. . ." Twitter post, November 25, 2022b. As of November 28, 2022: https://twitter.com/RobinBrooksIIF/status/1596211454025388038

Business Wire, "Clinton Bush Haiti Fund Invests to Complete Construction of Haitian-Owned Hotel and Conference Center in Port au Prince," May 9, 2011.

Cabinet Office of Japan, "Gross Domestic Expenditure at Constant Prices (Fiscal Year)," Economic and Social Research, webpage, undated. As of November 4, 2022:
https://www.esri.cao.go.jp/en/sna/data/sokuhou/files/2001/qe011/gdemenuea.html

Calmes, Jackie, "Lew Defends Sanctions, but Cautions on Overuse," *New York Times*, March 29, 2016.

Cancian, Mark F., "Aid to Ukraine Explained in Six Charts," Center for Strategic and International Studies, November 18, 2022.

Center for Nations in Transition, Hubert H. Humphrey Institute of Public Affairs, *Final Report of the Environmental Training Project; U.S. Agency for International Development Cooperative Agreement EUR-0041-A-00-2020*, University of Minnesota, Center for Hazardous Materials Research, Institute for Sustainable Communities, and the World Wildlife Fund, September 2001.

Charap, Samuel, and Michael J. Mazarr, "The Wisdom of U.S. Restraint on Russia," *Foreign Affairs*, September 12, 2022.

Charap, Samuel, and Timothy J. Colton, *Everyone Loses: The Ukraine Crisis and the Ruinous Contest for Post-Soviet Eurasia*, Routledge, 2017.

Clancy, Noreen, Melissa L. Finucane, Jordan R. Fischbach, David G. Groves, Debra Knopman, Karishma V. Patel, and Lloyd Dixon, *The Building Resilient Infrastructure and Communities Mitigation Grant Program: Incorporating Hazard Risk and Social Equity into Decisionmaking Processes*, Homeland Security Operational Analysis Center operated by the RAND Corporation, RR-A1258-1, 2022. As of April 5, 2023:
https://www.rand.org/pubs/research_reports/RRA1258-1.html

Cohen, Jerome B., "Table IV-2, Indexes of Japanese Industrial Production, 1946, 1948, 1950–1956," in *Japan's Postwar Economy*, Indiana University Press, 1958.

Cole, David C., and Princeton N. Lyman, *Korean Development: The Interplay of Politics and Economics*, Harvard University Press, 1971.

Congressional Research Service, "Summary: S.2532—102nd Congress (1991–1992): Conference Report Filed in House," October 1, 1992.

Conley, Heather A., *A Modern Marshall Plan for Ukraine: Seven Lessons from History to Deliver Hope*, German Marshall Fund of the United States, October 3, 2022,

Constant, Louay, Shelly Culbertson, Jonathan S. Blake, Mary Kate Adgie, and Hardika Dayalani, *In Search of a Durable Solution: Examining the Factors Influencing Postconflict Refugee Returns*, RAND Corporation, RR-A1327-1, 2021. As of March 28, 2023:
https://www.rand.org/pubs/research_reports/RRA1327-1.html

Controller and Auditor-General, *Canterbury Earthquake Recovery Authority: Assessing Its Effectiveness and Efficiency*, New Zealand House of Representatives, 2017.

Cook, Cynthia, "Rebuilding Ukraine After the War," Center for Strategic and International Studies, March 2, 2022.

Council on Foreign Relations, "'The Marshall Plan: Dawn of the Cold War' by Benn Steil," webpage, February 13, 2018. As of November 4, 2022: https://www.cfr.org/event/marshall-plan-dawn-cold-war-benn-steil

Courtney, William, Khrystyna Holynska, and Howard J. Shatz, "Tackling Corruption Is Key to Rebuilding Ukraine," United Press International, April 18, 2022.

Culbertson, Shelly, and Charles Ries, "Ukraine Invasion Could Spark a Massive Refugee Crisis," *Newsweek*, February 16, 2022.

Culbertson, Shelly, Blas Nuñez-Neto, Joie D. Acosta, Cynthia R. Cook, Andrew Lauland, Kristin J. Leuschner, Shanthi Nataraj, Benjamin Lee Preston, Susan A. Resetar, Adam C. Resnick, Patrick Roberts, and Howard J. Shatz, *Recovery in the U.S. Virgin Islands: Progress, Challenges, and Options for the Future*, Homeland Security Operational Analysis Center operated by the RAND Corporation, RR-A282-1, 2020. As of March 28, 2023: https://www.rand.org/pubs/research_reports/RRA282-1.html

Culbertson, Shelly, John Bordeaux, Italo A. Gutierrez, Andrew Lauland, Kristin J. Leuschner, Blas Nuñez-Neto, and Lisa Saum-Manning, *Building Back Locally: Supporting Puerto Rico's Municipalities in Post-Hurricane Reconstruction*, Homeland Security Operational Analysis Center operated by the RAND Corporation, RR-3041-DHS, 2020. As of March 28, 2023: https://www.rand.org/pubs/research_reports/RR3041.html

Culbertson, Shelly, Olga Oliker, Ben Baruch, and Ilana Blum, *Rethinking Coordination of Services to Refugees in Urban Areas: Managing the Crisis in Jordan and Lebanon*, RAND Corporation, RR-1485-DOS, 2016. As of March 28, 2023: https://www.rand.org/pubs/research_reports/RR1485.html

Currie, Chris, *Update on FEMA's Disaster Recovery Efforts in Puerto Rico and the U.S. Virgin Islands*, testimony before the Subcommittee on Economic Development, Public Buildings, and Emergency Management, House of Representatives, September 15, 2022a.

Currie, Chris, *Disaster Recovery: Actions Needed to Improve the Federal Approach*, Government Accountability Office, GAO-23-104956, November 15, 2022b.

Davis, Donald R., and David E. Weinstein, "Bombs, Bones, and Break Points: The Geography of Economic Activity," *American Economic Review*, Vol. 92, No. 5, December 2002.

De Long, J. Bradford, and Barry Eichengreen, "The Marshall Plan: History's Most Successful Structural Adjustment Program," National Bureau of Economic Research, Working Paper No. 3899, November 1991.

Diaspora Emergency Action and Coordination Platform, *Diaspora Organizations and Their Humanitarian Response in Ukraine,* U.S. Agency for International Development and Danish Refugee Council, July 2021.

DiPippo, Gerard, "Deterrence First: Applying Lessons from Sanctions on Russia to China," Center for Strategic and International Studies, May 3, 2022.

Dobbins, James, Seth G. Jones, Keith Crane, Christopher S. Chivvis, Andrew Radin, F. Stephen Larrabee, Nora Bensahel, Brooke K. Stearns, and Benjamin W. Goldsmith, *Europe's Role in Nation-Building: From the Balkans to the Congo,* RAND Corporation, MG-722-RC, 2008. As of March 28, 2023: https://www.rand.org/pubs/monographs/MG722.html

Dobbins, James, John G. McGinn, Keith Crane, Seth G. Jones, Rollie Lal, Andrew Rathmell, Rachel M. Swanger, and Anga R. Timilsina, *America's Role in Nation-Building: From Germany to Iraq,* RAND Corporation, MR-1753-RC, 2003. As of March 28, 2023: https://www.rand.org/pubs/monograph_reports/MR1753.html

Dunn, Amina, "As Russian Invasion Nears One-Year Mark, Partisans Grow Further Apart on U.S. Support for Ukraine," Pew Research Center, January 31, 2023.

Eastham, Steve, David Cowles, and Richard Johnson, *The Enterprise Funds in Europe and Eurasia: Successes and Lessons Learned,* U.S. Agency for International Development, September 12, 2013.

Erlanger, Steven, "What Does It Mean to Provide 'Security Guarantees' to Ukraine?" *New York Times,* January 10, 2023.

Evenett, Simon, "Trade Policy and Deterring War: The Case of Ukraine Since the Annexation of Crimea," Global Trade Alert, February 14, 2022.

European Bank for Reconstruction and Development, "The History of the EBRD," webpage, undated. As of November 7, 2022: https://www.ebrd.com/who-we-are/history-of-the-ebrd.html

European Commission, "President Juncker Appoints Michel Barnier as Chief Negotiator in Charge of the Preparation and Conduct of the Negotiations with the United Kingdom Under Article 50 of the TEU," press release, July 27, 2016.

European Commission, France, Germany, Italy, the United Kingdom, Canada, and the United States, "Joint Statement on Further Restrictive Economic Measures," February 26, 2022.

European Parliament, "Parliament Approves €18 Billion Loan for Ukraine for 2023," press release, November 24, 2022.

Fearon, James D., "Rationalist Explanations for War," *International Organization*, Vol. 49, No. 3, Summer 1995.

Federal Emergency Management Agency, "Mission Areas and Core Capabilities," webpage, last updated July 20, 2020a. As of April 5, 2023: https://www.fema.gov/emergency-managers/national-preparedness/mission-core-capabilities

Federal Emergency Management Agency, "Community Lifelines," webpage, last updated July 27, 2020b. As of December 18, 2022: https://www.fema.gov/emergency-managers/practitioners/lifelines

FEMA—*See* Federal Emergency Management Agency.

Ford, Jess, and A. H. Huntington III, *Enterprise Funds' Contributions to Private Sector Development Vary*, U.S. General Accounting Office, GAO/NSIAD-99-221, September 1999.

Fortna, Virginia Page, "Scraps of Paper? Agreements and the Durability of Peace," *International Organization*, Vol. 57, No. 2, 2003.

Frederick, Bryan, Samuel Charap, Scott Boston, Stephen J. Flanagan, Michael J. Mazarr, Jennifer D. P. Moroney, and Karl P. Mueller, *Pathways to Russian Escalation Against NATO from the Ukraine War*, RAND Corporation, PE-A1971-1, 2022. As of March 28, 2023: https://www.rand.org/pubs/perspectives/PEA1971-1.html

Fukui, Haruhiko, "Economic Planning in Postwar Japan: A Case Study in Policy Making," *Asian Survey*, Vol. 12, No. 4, April 1972.

Galushko, Vladyslav, Iskra Kirova, Inna Pidluska, and Daniela Schwarzer, *War and Peace: Supporting Ukraine to Prevail, Rebuild, and Prosper*, Open Society Foundations, October 2022.

Gamboa, Suzanne, "Puerto Rico's Population Fell 11.8% to 3.3 Million, Census Shows," NBC News, April 26, 2021.

Ganster, Ronja, Jacob Kirkegaard, Thomas Kleine-Brockhoff, and Bruce Stokes, *Designing Ukraine's Recovery in the Spirit of the Marshall Plan: Principles, Architecture, Financing, Accountability: Recommendations for Donor Countries*, German Marshall Fund of the United States, September 2022.

Germanovich, Gene, "Finnish and Swedish NATO Membership: Toward a Larger, Stronger, Smarter Alliance," United Press International, August 12, 2022.

Gijs, Camille, "Zelenskyy: Ukraine Ready to Discuss Neutral Status to Reach Russia Peace Deal," *Politico*, March 28, 2022.

Gligorov, Vladimir, Mary Kaldor, and Loukas Tsoukalis, *Balkan Reconstruction and European Integration*, Hellenic Observatory, Centre for the Study of Global Governance, and Vienna Institute for International Economic Studies, October 1999.

Gorodnichenko, Yuriy, Ilona Sologoub, and Beatrice Weder di Mauro, eds., *Rebuilding Ukraine: Principles and Policies*, Centre for Economic Policy Research, November 2022.

Governor of Puerto Rico and Central Office of Recovery, Reconstruction, and Resiliency, *Transformation and Innovation in the Wake of Recovery: An Economic and Recovery Plan for Puerto Rico*, August 2018.

"Gross Domestic Product as a Measure of U.S. Production," *Survey of Current Business*, Vol. 71, No. 8, August 1991.

Hamada, Koichi, and Munehisa Kasuya, "The Reconstruction and Stabilization of the Postwar Japanese Economy: Possible Lessons for Eastern Europe," Center Discussion Paper No. 672, Economic Growth Center, Yale University, 1992.

Harrell, Peter, "How to Hit Russia Where It Hurts," *Foreign Affairs*, January 3, 2019.

Helsinki Commission Staff, *The Internal Enemy: A Helsinki Commission Staff Report on Corruption in Ukraine*, Commission on Security and Cooperation in Europe, October 2017.

Hill, John S., "American Efforts to Aid French Reconstruction Between Lend-Lease and the Marshall Plan," *Journal of Modern History*, Vol. 64, No. 3, September 1992.

Holynska, Khrystyna, Jay Balagna, and Krystyna Marcinek, *Fighting for the Future: The Tradeoff's in Ukraine's Recovery*, RAND Corporation, RR-A2370-1, 2023. As of May 25, 2023:
https://www.rand.org/pubs/research_reports/RRA2370-1.html

Hurricane Sandy Rebuilding Task Force, *Hurricane Sandy Rebuilding Strategy: Strong Communities, A Resilient Region*, August 2013.

International Monetary Fund, *Ukraine: First Review Under the Stand-By Arrangement, Requests for Extension and Rephasing of Access of the Arrangement, Waiver of Nonobservance of a Performance Criterion, Financing Assurances Review, and Monetary Policy Consultation*, IMF Country Report No. 21/250, November 8, 2021.

International Monetary Fund, *World Economic Outlook: Countering the Cost-of-Living Crisis*, October 2022a.

International Monetary Fund, "How Ukraine Is Managing a War Economy," December 22, 2022b.

International Monetary Fund, "Currency Composition of Official Foreign Exchange Reserves (COFER)," webpage, last updated December 23, 2022c. As of February 14, 2023:
https://data.imf.org/?sk=E6A5F467-C14B-4AA8-9F6D-5A09EC4E62A4

International Organization for Migration, *Ukraine—Internal Displacement Report—General Population Survey Round 12 (16–23 January 2023)*, February 2, 2023.

International Republican Institute, "Research from Four Cities in Ukraine Highlights Importance of Decentralization," November 8, 2019.

"Iraq Makes Final Reparation Payment to Kuwait for 1990 Invasion," UN News, February 9, 2022.

Istomina, Toma, "Ukraine Ends 2019 with Smaller Budget Deficit Than Expected," *Kyiv Post*, January 3, 2020.

"Japanese Yen Pegged at Rate of 360 for $1," *New York Times*, April 23, 1949.

Jarábik, Balázs, and Yulia Yesmukhanova, "Ukraine's Slow Struggle for Decentralization," Carnegie Endowment for International Peace, March 8, 2017.

Jervis, Robert, "Cooperation Under the Security Dilemma," *World Politics*, Vol. 30, No. 2, January 1978.

Johnson, David E., "This Is What the Russians Do," *Lawfire* blog, Duke University, May 3, 2022. As of November 28, 2022:
https://sites.duke.edu/lawfire/2022/05/03/dr-dave-johnsons-warning-on-brute-force-in-the-ukraine-this-is-what-the-russians-do/

Jones, Claire, and Joseph Cotterill, "Russia's FX Reserves Slip from Its Grasp," *Financial Times*, February 28, 2022.

Kaminski, Bartlomiej, "The Europe Agreements and Transition: Unique Returns from Integrating into the European Union," in Sorin Antohi and Vladimir Tisaneanu, eds., *Between Past and Future: The Revolutions of 1989 and Their Aftermath*, Central European University Press, 2000.

Karazy, Sergiy, "Almost One Third of Ukraine Needs to Be Cleared of Ordnance, Ministry Says," Reuters, August 12, 2022.

Kintsurashvili, Konstantine, and Ana Kresic, *Ukraine Diagnostic*, European Bank for Reconstruction and Development, December 2018.

Kortunov, Andrey, "Is a Marshall Plan for Ukraine Possible?" Russian International Affairs Council, November 3, 2022.

KSE Institute, Ministry of Community Development and Territories of Ukraine, Ministry of Infrastructure of Ukraine, and Ministry of Health of Ukraine, *Assessment of Damages in Ukraine Due to Russia's Military Aggression as of September 1, 2022*, September 2022.

Lawder, David, "Yellen Says Legal Obstacles Remain on Seizure of Russian Assets to Aid Ukraine," Reuters, February 27, 2023.

Leffler, Melvyn P., "The United States and the Strategic Dimensions of the Marshall Plan," *Diplomatic History*, Vol. 12, No. 3, Summer 1988.

Leonhardt, David, "Three War Scenarios," *New York Times*, July 6, 2022.

Lewarne, Stephen, Nell Todd, Joe Mariani, Joniel Sung-Jin Cha, and Stuart Williamson, "The Reconstruction of Ukraine: Historical Lessons for Postwar Reconstruction of Ukraine," Deloitte, October 10, 2022.

Lichfield, Charles, "Windfall: How Russia Managed Oil and Gas Income After Invading Ukraine, and How It Will Have to Make Do with Less," Atlantic Council, November 30, 2022.

Lugano Declaration: Outcome Document of the Ukraine Recovery Conference URC2022, Ukraine Recovery Conference, July 5, 2022.

Mankiw, N. Gregory, "Ukraine: How Not to Run an Economy," *Fortune*, June 12, 2000.

Marks, Sally, "The Myth of Reparations," *Central European History*, Vol. 11, No. 3, September 1978.

Massicot, Dara, "Russia's Repeat Failures: Moscow's New Strategy in Ukraine Is Just as Bad as the Old One," *Foreign Affairs*, August 15, 2022.

Mazarr, Michael J., *Understanding Deterrence*, RAND Corporation, PE-295-RC, 2018. As of April 3, 2023:
https://www.rand.org/pubs/perspectives/PE295.html

Minakov, Mykhailo, "Three Decades of Ukraine's Independence," *Focus Ukraine* blog, Kennan Institute, September 13, 2021. As of December 16, 2022:
https://www.wilsoncenter.org/blog-post/
three-decades-ukraines-independence

Moroney, Jennifer D. P., James A. Schear, Joie D. Acosta, Chandra Garber, Sarah Heintz, Jeffrey W. Hornung, Yun Kang, Samantha McBirney, Richard E. Neiman, Jr., Stephanie Pezard, David E. Thaler, and Teddy Ulin, *International Postdisaster Recoveries: Lessons for Puerto Rico on Supply-Chain Management and Recovery Governance*, Homeland Security Operational Analysis Center operated by the RAND Corporation, RR-3042-DHS, 2020. As of April 3, 2023:
https://www.rand.org/pubs/research_reports/RR3042.html

Multilateral Investment Guarantee Agency, "What We Do," webpage, undated. As of February 13, 2023:
https://www.miga.org/what-we-do

Nardelli, Alberto, "EU Urged to Make Banks Report Size of Frozen Russian Assets," Bloomberg, February 9, 2023.

National Centers for Environmental Information, "Costliest U.S. Tropical Cyclones," fact sheet, National Oceanic and Atmospheric Administration, 2022.

National Recovery Council, *Ukraine's National Recovery Plan*, presentation, Ukraine Recovery Conference, July 2022.

NATO—*See* North Atlantic Treaty Organization.

North Atlantic Treaty Organization, "Bucharest Summit Declaration," April 3, 2008.

Office of the Historian, U.S. Foreign Service Institute, "The Dawes Plan, the Young Plan, German Reparations, and Inter-Allied War Debts," webpage, U.S. Department of State, undated. As of February 14, 2023: https://history.state.gov/milestones/1921-1936/dawes

Office of the President of Ukraine, "Andriy Yermak and Anders Fogh Rasmussen Jointly Present Recommendations on Security Guarantees of Ukraine," September 13, 2022.

Organisation for Economic Co-operation and Development, *Harmonising Donor Practices for Effective Aid Delivery*, 2003.

Padgett, Tim, "Haiti's Quake, One Year Later: It's the Rubble, Stupid!" *Time*, January 12, 2011.

Patel, Neil, "How to End the Ukraine War," *Daily Caller*, February 23, 2023.

Patten, Chris, *Not Quite the Diplomat: Home Truths About World Affairs*, Allen Lane, 2005.

Pettis, Michael, "Will the Chinese Renminbi Replace the US Dollar?" *Review of Keynesian Economics*, Vol. 10, No. 4, Winter 2022.

Plyer, Allison, "Facts for Features: Katrina Impact," Data Center, webpage, August 26, 2016. As of April 5, 2023: https://www.datacenterresearch.org/data-resources/katrina/facts-for-impact/

de Pommereau, Isabelle, "Germany Finishes Paying WWI Reparations, Ending Century of 'Guilt,'" *Christian Science Monitor*, October 4, 2010.

Public Law 101-179, Support for Eastern European Democracy (SEED) Act of 1989, November 28, 1989.

Public Law 102-511, Freedom for Russia and Emerging Eurasian Democracies and Open Markets Support Act of 1992, October 24, 1992.

Public Law 115-123, Bipartisan Budget Act of 2018, February 9, 2018.

Public Law 117-328, Consolidated Appropriations Act, 2023, December 29, 2022.

Queensland Reconstruction Authority, *2010/11 Queensland Flood and Cyclone Disaster: Value for Money Strategy*, Queensland Government, undated.

Ramey, Kelly, "The Changeover from GNP to GDP: A Milestone in BEA History," *Survey of Current Business*, Vol. 101, No. 3, March 2021.

RAND Corporation, *Mass Migration: How RAND Is Addressing One of the Greatest Challenges and Opportunities of the Century*, CP-A715-1, 2020. As of April 5, 2023:
https://www.rand.org/pubs/corporate_pubs/CPA715-1.html

Reach, Clint, "Obstacles to Lasting Peace Between Ukraine and Russia," *Santa Monica Daily Press*, July 7, 2022.

Reinhard, Scott, "Ukraine Has Reclaimed More Than Half the Territory Russia Has Taken This Year," *New York Times*, November 14, 2022.

Repko, Maria, "Financing Ukraine's Victory and Recovery: For the War and Beyond," Stockholm Centre for Eastern European Studies, blog post, November 17, 2022. As of November 28, 2022:
https://sceeus.se/en/publications/
financing-ukraines-victory-and-recovery-for-the-war-and-beyond/

Reynolds, Garfield, "Pozsar Says $300 Billion Russia Cash Pile Can Roil Money Markets," Bloomberg, February 24, 2022.

Roaf, James, Ruben Atoyan, Bikas Joshi, and Krzysztof Krogulsi, *25 Years of Transition: Post-Communist Europe and the IMF*, International Monetary Fund, Regional Economic Issues Special Report, October 2014.

Rudolph, Joshua, and Norman L. Eisen, "Ukraine's Anti-Corruption Fight Can Overcome US Skeptics," *Just Security*, November 10, 2022.

Rumer, Eugene, and Richard Sokolsky, "Putin's War Against Ukraine and the Balance of Power in Europe," Carnegie Endowment for International Peace, April 11, 2022.

Rustamova, Farida, "Ukraine's 10-Point Plan," *Faridaily* blog, March 29, 2022. As of April 3, 2023:
https://faridaily.substack.com/p/ukraines-10-point-plan

Sachs, Jeffrey, "Progress of Economic Reform in Eastern Europe," presentation, College of Saint Benedict and Saint John's University, Clemens Lecture Series No. 5, October 3, 1991.

Sachs, Jeffrey, "Shock Therapy in Poland: Perspectives of Five Years," presentation, University of Utah, Tanner Lectures on Human Values, April 7, 1994.

Sachs, Jeffrey, and David Lipton, "Poland's Economic Reform," *Foreign Affairs*, Vol. 69, No. 3, Summer 1990.

SALT, "Benn Steil: 'The Marshall Plan: Dawn of the Cold War,' SALT Talks 137," webpage, January 11, 2021. As of November 4, 2022: https://www.salt.org/talks/library/benn-steil-137

Serafino, Nina, Curt Tarnoff, and Dick K. Nanto, *U.S. Occupation Assistance: Iraq, Germany and Japan Compared*, Congressional Research Service, RL33331, March 23, 2006.

Schelling, Thomas, *Arms and Influence*, Yale University Press, 2008.

Schlichter, Kurt, "Ukraine's Friends May Doom It—and Us," *Townhall*, February 23, 2023.

Shapiro, Jeremy, James Dobbins, Yauheni Preiherman, Pernille Rieker, and Andrei Zagorski, "Regional Security Architecture," in Samuel Charap, Jeremy Shapiro, John Drennan, Oleksandr Chalyi, Reinhard Krumm, Yulia Nikitina, and Gwendolyn Sasse, eds., *A Consensus Proposal for a Revised Regional Order in Post-Soviet Europe and Eurasia*, RAND Corporation, CF-410-CC, 2019. As of April 3, 2023: https://www.rand.org/pubs/conf_proceedings/CF410.html

Shatz, Howard J., and Nathan Chandler, *Global Economic Trends and the Future of Warfare: The Changing Environment and Its Implications for the U.S. Air Force*, RAND Corporation, RR-2849/4-AF, 2020. As of April 3, 2023: https://www.rand.org/pubs/research_reports/RR2849z4.html

Society for Worldwide Interbank Financial Transactions, "RMB Tracker," webpage, undated. As of February 14, 2023: https://www.swift.com/our-solutions/compliance-and-shared-services/business-intelligence/renminbi/rmb-tracker/rmb-tracker-document-centre

Steil, Benn, *The Marshall Plan: Dawn of the Cold War*, Oxford University Press, 2018.

Steil, Benn, "No Marshall Plan for Ukraine: Geography and Geopolitics Dictate a Different Reconstruction Model," *Foreign Affairs*, May 13, 2022.

Steil, Benn, "Why It Is So Hard to Repeat the Marshall Plan," German Marshall Fund of the United States, June 6, 2022.

Steil, Benn, and Benjamin Della Rocca, "It Takes More Than Money to Make a Marshall Plan," *Geo-Graphics* blog, Council on Foreign Relations, April 9, 2018. As of January 17, 2023: https://www.cfr.org/blog/it-takes-more-money-make-marshall-plan

Stephan, Paul, "Giving Russian Assets to Ukraine – Freezing is not Seizing," *Lawfare* blog, April 26, 2022.

Sutela, Pekka, *The Underachiever: Ukraine's Economy Since 1991*, Carnegie Endowment for International Peace, March 2012.

Suzuki, Yoshio, "Difficulties and Challenges: Japan's Post-War History of Economic Trends and Monetary Policy," Center on Japanese Economy and Business, Columbia Business School, Working Paper Series No. 360, August 2017.

Tarnoff, Curt, *The Former Soviet Union and U.S. Foreign Assistance in 1992: The Role of Congress,* Congressional Research Service, RL32410, May 20, 2004.

Tarnoff, Curt, *The Marshall Plan: Design, Accomplishments, and Significance,* Congressional Research Service, R45079, January 18, 2018.

Teasdale, Anthony, and Timothy Bainbridge, "Europe Agreement," *Penguin Companion to European Union,* webpage, October 1, 2012. As of November 28, 2022:
https://penguincompaniontoeu.com/additional_entries/europe-agreements/

Temnycky, Mark, "A Marshall Plan for Ukraine," Center for European Policy Analysis, May 25, 2022.

Timilsina, Anga R., and James Dobbins, "Shaping the Policy Priorities for Post-Conflict Reconstruction," *Policy Insight,* Vol. 1, No. 5, CP-521-(10/07), 2007.

Transparency International, "Transparency International Releases the Year 2000 Corruption Perceptions Index. New Index Is Based on Multiple Surveys from 1998–2000," press release, September 12, 2000.

Transparency International, *Corruption Perceptions Index 2010,* September 30, 2010.

Transparency International, *Corruption Perceptions Index 2020,* January 28, 2021.

Troianovski, Anton, and Julian E. Barnes, "Russian Invasion of Ukraine: 'The Work Is Going Smoothly': Putin Suggests That He Can Outlast Ukraine and the West," *New York Times,* June 30, 2022.

United Nations, "UN Comtrade Database," undated. As of February 13, 2023:
https://comtrade.un.org/

United Nations, *Statistical Yearbook 1956,* No. 8, Statistical Office of the United Nations, Department of Economic and Social Affairs, 1956.

United Nations, High Commissioner for Refugees, "Operational Data Portal: Ukraine Refugee Situation," webpage, undated. As of December 16, 2022:
https://data.unhcr.org/en/situations/ukraine

United Nations, Office for Disaster Risk Reduction, *Build Back Better: In Recovery, Rehabilitation, and Reconstruction (Consultative Version),* 2017.

"United Nations Rehabilitation and Relief Administration," *International Organization,* Vol. 3, No. 3, August 1949.

Urwin, Derek W., *The Community of Europe: A History of European Integration Since 1945*, 2nd ed., Routledge, 1995.

U.S. Agency for International Development, "Europe and Eurasia," webpage, undated. As of December 18, 2022:
https://www.usaid.gov/where-we-work/europe-eurasia

U.S. Agency for International Development, "USAID: Partners for Financial Stability (PFS) Program," fact sheet, revised January 20, 2004.

U.S. Agency for International Development, "A U.S.-Supported E-Government App Accelerated the Digital Transformation of Ukraine; Now Ukraine Is Working to Scale the Solution to More Countries," press release, January 18, 2023.

USAID—*See* U.S. Agency for International Development.

U.S. Bureau of Economic Analysis, "Current-Dollar and 'Real' Gross Domestic Product," spreadsheet, October 27, 2022a.

U.S. Bureau of Economic Analysis, "National Income and Product Accounts: Table 1.1.9. Implicit Price Deflators for Gross Domestic Product," interactive data file, last revised on December 22, 2022b.

U.S. Census Bureau, "Current Versus Constant (or Real) Dollars," webpage, last revised September 12, 2022. As of January 17, 2022:
https://www.census.gov/topics/income-poverty/income/guidance/current-vs-constant-dollars.html

U.S. Census Bureau, "International Database: World Population Estimates and Projections," webpage, last revised December 21, 2021. As of February 3, 2023:
https://www.census.gov/programs-surveys/international-programs/about/idb.html

Van Schaick, F., "Conditions for American Aid," *Congressional Quarterly Editorial Research Reports*, Vol. 2, October 17, 1947.

Verbyany, Volodymyr, "Ukrainian Inflation Tops 23% as Prices Surge for Seventh Month," *Bloomberg*, September 9, 2022.

Vimont, Pierre, "Ukraine's Indispensable Economic Reforms," Carnegie Europe, April 29, 2016.

Weiss, Martin A., *European Bank for Reconstruction and Development (EBRD)*, IF11419, Congressional Research Service, updated November 9, 2022.

Werner, Suzanne, "The Precarious Nature of Peace: Resolving the Issues, Enforcing the Settlement, and Renegotiating the Terms," *American Journal of Political Science*, Vol. 43, No. 3, July 1999.

White House, "Remarks by President Biden on Russia's Unprovoked and Unjustified Attack on Ukraine," February 24, 2022.

"Why the West Should Be Wary of Permanently Seizing Russian Assets," *The Economist*, June 9, 2022.

World Bank, *From Plan to Market: World Development Report 1996*, Oxford University Press, 1996.

World Bank, *Transition: The First Ten Years: Analysis and Lessons for Eastern Europe and the Former Soviet Union*, 2002.

World Bank, "World Development Indicators," database, December 22, 2022. As of February 5, 2023:
https://databank.worldbank.org/source/world-development-indicators

World Bank, "Trust Funds and Programs," webpage, 2023. As of February 13, 2023:
https://www.worldbank.org/en/programs/trust-funds-and-programs

World Bank, the Government of Ukraine, and the European Commission, *Ukraine: Rapid Damage and Needs Assessment*, July 31, 2022.

Zanardi, Louis H., Michael J. Courts, Bruce L. Kutnick, Muriel J. Forster, Bill J. Keller, John D. DeForge, and Walter E. Bayer, Jr., *Poland: Economic Restructuring and Donor Assistance*, General Accounting Office, GAO/NSIAD-95-150, August 1995.

Zarate, Juan C., "Sanctions and Financial Pressure: Major National Security Tools," testimony before the U.S. House of Representatives Foreign Affairs Committee, January 10, 2018.

Zelensky, Volodymyr, "Invest in the Future of Ukraine," *Wall Street Journal*, September 5, 2022.

Zelikow, Philip, and Simon Johnson, "How Ukraine Can Build Back Better: Use the Kremlin's Seized Assets to Pay for Reconstruction," *Foreign Affairs*, April 19, 2022.

Zink, Richard, "The EU and Reconstruction in the Western Balkans," in Jean Dufourcq and David S. Yost, eds., *NATO-EU Cooperation in Post Conflict Reconstruction*, NATO Defense College, NDC Occasional Paper 15, May 2006.

Zoellick, Robert B., "How the G-7 Can Tip the Scales Toward Ukraine," *Washington Post*, June 26, 2022a.

Zoellick, Robert B., "Russian Cash Can Keep Ukraine Alive This Winter," *Wall Street Journal*, October 26, 2022b.

Zweers, Wouter, Giulia Cretti, Myrthe de Bon, Alban Dafa, Strahinja Subotić, Milena Muk, Arber Fetahu, Ardita Abazi Imeri, Emina Kuhinja, and Hata Kujraković, *The EU as a Promoter of Democracy or 'Stabilitocracy' in the Western Balkans?* Clingendael Institute and the Think for Europe Network, February 2022.